THE PAST, LOVE, MONEY AND MUCH MORE

THE PAST, LOVE, MONEY AND MUCH MORE

Philippines-Japan Relations Since the End of the Second World War

EDITED BY

Lydia N. Yu Jose

Japanese Studies Program

Japanese Studies Program
School of Social Sciences, Loyola Schools
Leong Hall, Ateneo de Manila University
Loyola Heights, Quezon City
P.O. Box 154, Manila 1099
Telephone: 4266001 loc. 5248

Cover and book design by Karl Fredrick M. Castro

The National Library of the Philippines CIP Data

Recommended entry:

The past, love, money and much more : Philippines-
Japan relations since the end of the Second World War /
edited by Lydia N. Yu Jose. – Quezon City : Japanese
Studies Program, Ateneo de Manila University, 2008.
p. ; cm.

1. Philippines—Relations—Japan. 2. Philippines—Foreign
relations—Japan. 3. Cultural relations. I. Yu Jose, Lydia N.

DS673.J3 303.482'599'052 2008 P081000014
ISBN 978-971-0426-03-4

Contents

Acknowledgments

CHAPTERS 1, 3, AND 5 THROUGH EIGHT OF THIS BOOK WERE SELECTED from among the papers presented at the international conference on "RP-Japan Relations: Love, Money, Environment, and Much More," organized by the Japanese Studies Program of the Ateneo de Manila University on 10 to 12 May 2006. The conference was supported by the Japan Foundation, Manila. Before Chapter 1 was presented to the conference on love, money, environment and much more, a much longer version was first read at the international conference on "Globalization, Localization, and Japanese Studies in the Asia-Pacific Region," organized by the International Research Center for Japanese Studies, more popularly known in Japanese as Nichibunken and the Department of Japanese Studies of the Chinese University of Hong Kong, held in Hong Kong on 30 September to 4 October 2005. Chapter 2, on the other hand, is pretty much the same paper I presented at the international conference on "Japan's Asian Strategy and Her Soft Power," organized by Keio University in Tokyo from 23 to 25 October 2006. Chapter 9 was originally a paper with a larger theme presented in an international conference on "Japan: A Reintroduction," organized by the Japanese Studies Program of the Ateneo on 12 to 14 May 2005, with support from the Japan Foundation (Tokyo).

I am deeply grateful to the Nichibunken and Keio University for giving me permission to publish Chapter 1 and Chapter 2, respectively. Special thanks go to the Japan Foundation (Manila and Tokyo) for the support it gave to the conference which is the provenance of more than half of the chapters that comprise this book, and the conference from where I got Chapter 9.

To complete the theme and argument I was trying to construct, I asked my colleagues and graduate students for good papers that have not been published, and fortunately, I got two that fit the theme in my mind. Chapter 10 was a term paper written by a student of mine in Philippines-Japan Relations in the school year 2003–2004, and Chapter 11 was culled from my advisee's M.A. thesis. He successfully defended it in May 2007. I thank them for wholeheartedly entrusting their papers to me.

I did not work alone on the papers and the theme. My colleagues graciously agreed to review the manuscripts, resulting in eliminations, additions, restoration of what had been eliminated, eliminating what had originally been accepted, and so on. Even though I cannot mention the names of the reviewers because we followed a blind system of review, I would like to express my deep appreciation for the helpful comments they gave.

A note on Japanese names. Japanese names are written according to the traditional practice of writing the surname first, followed by the given name.

Introduction

The Philippines and Japan: Not so Unequal, After All

Lydia N. Yu Jose

This book revises the common observation that Philippines-Japan relations are characterized by inequality. Such an observation is the twin of another common observation, that the bilateral relationship between the Philippines and Japan is largely economic in nature. We tentatively accept the observation that Philippines-Japan relations are mainly economic. We also accept the observation that it is a relationship between a developed country and a developing one. But we argue that to say that it is an unequal relationship is to say nothing of significance, because, naturally, the relationship between a developed and a developing country is unequal.

For two countries that have had relations for more than a century, there is certainly something more that can be said about this relationship, aside from the obvious. We can arrive at a more significant and nuanced characterization of Philippines-Japan relations by looking at the other aspects of the relationship without totally dismissing the admittedly important economic relationship. As we conditionally admit that the relationship is unequal, we look at the balance to see which side is heavier; we change the contents of the balance and vary their combinations to find out if one side is always heavier than the other or if both sides are sometimes equal.

We will do this by narrating how the past is remembered, by bridging the elite and the popular, and by describing people-to-people relations across national borders within and beyond state structure.

We look at the insistence of the past on inserting itself in the present. We bridge the elite and the popular by looking into the Japanese culture promoted by the Japanese government which normally reaches only the elite, and the Japanese images projected in television and movies, which reach the popular mass of Filipino viewers. We also bridge the elite and the popular by looking at interactions between peoples: Japanese NGOs and the poor among the Filipinos, Japanese husbands and Filipino wives, and vice versa.

THE LITERATURE THUS FAR

This book covers less than half of the complete history of our relations with Japan. We have had relations with Japan since ancient times. In fact, in 1998, when we celebrated the centennial of the declaration of Philippine independence, Japan joined in the celebration. It does not mean, however, that by 1998, we had had only a century of relations with Japan—it has been more than that. The long relationship had problems, but they did not result in extremely serious conflicts, until the Second World War broke out in 1941. Japan invaded the Philippines and occupied it until 1945. What used to be a long, largely friendly relationship became one between conqueror and conquered. This wartime relationship ended with the ratification of the San Francisco Peace Treaty by the Philippine Senate in July 1956.

The joint commemoration in 1998 resulted in a number of publications, testaments to the long history of Philippines-Japan relations. The two major books among them is *Philippines-Japan Relations* (Ateneo de Manila University Press, 2003) and *A Friendship of Two Suns* (Embassy of the Philippines in Japan, 1998). These books provide an excellent historical background for Philippines-Japan relations before 1956. They also provide scholarly insights into various aspects of the relationship since 1956, namely, the war reparations agreement and its implementation, bilateral trade, Japanese investment, Japanese official development assistance (ODA), and Filipino overseas workers in Japan.

These books have profited from various scholarly works on different periods of Philippines-Japan relations: * Saniel 1969; Ikehata and Jose, Ricardo 1999; Jose, Ricardo and Jose, Lydia 1997; Jose, Lydia 1999; Sato 1994 and its various aspects (Dela Cruz 1997; Goodman 1967a; Goodman 1967b; Ohno 1986; Yoshikawa 1991).

However, since the two major centennial publications cover an extensive period, there is not enough space for a deeper analysis of our relations with Japan since after the normalization of relations in 1956. The economic aspects, especially trade, investment, and ODA, as well as diplomatic exchanges are well covered, but not what are usually referred to as cultural relations, which can include almost everything outside of investments, trade, ODA, and diplomatic relations.

About this Book

We do not wish to repeat nor reinterpret aspects of our relations with Japan that have been written about in major publications. Rather, we wish to fill the gap that remains, essentially that of the evolving cultural relations between Japan and the Philippines.

Cultural relationship is a deep and broad concept that usually refers to aspects that are not economic and political. In the case of the Philippines and Japan, it includes all the activities undertaken by the Japan Information and Cultural Center and the Japan Foundation. To wit only the usual ones: scholarship and fellowship grants to study or do research in Japan, promotion of the Japanese language, holding of Japanese film festivals, ikebana or origami demonstrations, and sponsoring lectures on Japan. Cultural relations also include cultural influences naturally resulting from interactions among people, such as the interaction between a Japanese husband and his Filipino wife, a Filipina entertainer and a Japanese client, or a Filipino cook and his/her Japanese expatriate employer in the Philippines. And last but not least, it includes cultural influences resulting from mere exposure to Japanese goods, Japanese films (even those not sponsored by the Japan Foundation or any Japanese government agency), fashions, and the like.

The list is the same for the Philippines, but the fact is that cultural influences brought about by deliberate government efforts, like those exerted by the Japanese government, are limited in this country. Exposure of the Japanese people to Philippine goods, movies, and the like is very limited. The Philippines does not have a cultural center or an institution similar to the Japan Foundation that is endowed with resources to promote Philippine culture in Japan. Neither are Philippine goods in Japan half as widespread as Japanese cars, refrigerators, television sets, cameras, toys, gizmos, cartoons, and the like in the Philippines.

Japan is obviously much more capable of promoting its culture abroad, but imparting Philippine culture to Japan through person-to-person interaction is a different matter.

I have argued elsewhere that the movement of Filipinos and Japanese across their national borders is the most sustained and intense of all aspects of the relationship between the two peoples (Jose, Lydia 2003, 202–10). At present, Filipinos constitute the largest Southeast Asian population in Japan. Filipino-Japanese marriages are increasing, as are the number of *Japinos*, the more endearing version of which is *Japinoy*, a term that expresses the cultural influence of the Filipino language on English. Japino is short for Japanese-Filipino, child of a Japanese-Filipino couple. This refers to the young generation, and should not be confused with the older children of Japanese-Filipinos born before or during the Second World War. These children are called Nikkeijin (literally, Japanese descendants). That the older ones are known by their Japanese names and the younger ones by a coined word which is neither English nor Filipino, or can pass for either English or Filipino, indicates that the former were once hidden in Philippine society while the latter are very visible at present. When the Nikkeijin came out of hiding, so to speak, their attention was focused to Japan. They wanted to be recognized as Japanese citizens. The Japino, however, are clearly binational and bicultural.

The cultural relationship between the Philippines and Japan as a result of people-to-people interaction cannot therefore be dismissed as heavily Japanese. It is at least an interesting matter for investigation.

In this volume, we seek to understand cultural exchanges, interpretations, and images that occur or are formed in intercultural marriages between Filipinos and Japanese, in the interaction among Filipino and Japanese intellectuals, in the framework of Japanese NGOs operating in the Philippines, and in the popular medium of films. We focus primarily on people—Filipino and Japanese individuals who interact within given spheres of activities, actual as well as virtual. We include the spheres which are creations of the Japanese cultural policy, but we focus on the person-to-person interactions in these spheres, rather than the policies.

The Past, Love, and Money

We argue that the three elements which define Philippines-Japan relations since the end of the Second World War are history, love, and money. History refers to the past. Love refers to romantic attachments, both carnal and spiritual. It refers to the love between husband and wife, between lovers. It also refers to love of music and the arts, love of friends, love of learning, love of nature, including land. However, it does not refer to love of money and profit. Money refers to material, movable wealth, like cash, house, car, salary, loan, investment. It does not refer to wealth in general. The Philippines, for example, is rich in human and natural resources. When such wealth is considered, it would be hard to say that the Philippines is in a lower position in the so-called unequal relationship with Japan. The Philippines, however, does not have as much money as Japan has and in this respect it is definitely in a lower position.

Philippines-Japan relations since the end of the Second World War are inevitably enacted in the shadow of the immediate past: the war itself and the Japanese occupation of the Philippines. The past is in the present even though we are often oblivious of it. If we look hard enough, reminders of the Second World War are all around us. Some of them are visible in concrete and bronze, others exist only in our minds and hearts, and are occasionally given expression through ceremonies and rituals, as discussed in Chapter 1, "War Memorials and Commemorations in the Philippines, an Exploratory Look." Aside from memorials which are attempts by the living to remember the dead, there are old relics which have continued to exist and find a place, even usefulness, in the present—as in an old Second World War rampart used as a signpost (see gallery). And last but not least, the topic of the Japanese occupation is taught in schools and is written about in some books the children read (Jose, Lydia 2004; 2005).

The Second World War is also a favorite setting for movies, the Filipinos' most popular pastime. All, except one film discussed in Chapter 9, "The Japanese in the Filipino Cinematic Space," and chapter 10, "Gatas sa Dibdib ng Kaaway," are set in the Second World War. The legacy of the Second World War slowed down the progress of Japan's cultural policy towards the Philippines, as will be seen in Chapter 2, which discusses the development of Japan's cultural policy towards the Philippines and in Chapter 4, which narrates the growth of the first Japanese Studies Program in the Philippines. And last but not least, gathering of the bones of the war dead and visiting war memorials have become part of the project to attract Japanese tourists to the Philippines.

The Philippines can dig from the past a wealth of resources that it can use against Japan, if it wants to. Japan suffers from a poverty of resources from its past history of relations with the Philippines. From this standpoint, the relationship is indeed unequal, but tipped in favor of the Philippines. The question is, would the Philippines want to use the past to further its national interest vis-à-vis Japan?

Money—its possession, the lack of it, or the pursuit of it—is the other element that defines Philippines-Japan relations. Payment of war reparations after the war was of course about money, even though it was not supposed to be, but how could moral loss and the loss of lives be paid for? Soon after the ratification of the reparations agreement, Japan sought a treaty of amity, commerce and navigation. Despite the insertion of "amity," what the treaty sought was mainly trade and investment (Yoshikawa 2003), i.e., to use money to buy what Japan did not have but the Philippines had, to sell to the Philippines for profit, and to use capital to develop the natural resources of the Philippines, for more profit, of course.

The Treaty of Amity, Commerce, and Navigation was not ratified until December 1973. It was largely for the purpose of persuading the Philippines to ratify it that Japan embarked on a cultural policy in the 1960s. Chapter 2, "Japan's Cultural Diplomacy in the Last Fifty Years," argues that Japan used cultural diplomacy not only for its own sake but also to promote trade and investment. So intertwined are economics and cultural policy that the latter showed signs of success only in the 1980s, when incentives for it appeared in the form of job opportunities in Japan or in Japanese companies that relocated in the Philippines.

Money, or lack of it, is obvious in the present relationship between the Philippines and Japan. Japan has it, the Philippines does not. It was not as clear in the 1960s, when the Philippines was not so financially hard-up. A testament to this is the Asian Development Bank, created in the 1960s and located in the Philippines. In addition to the uphill climb of the Treaty of Amity, Commerce and Navigation, Japan failed in one of its earliest attempts to play a leading role in the Asian region. And the country that dealt the almost fatal blow was the Philippines.

In the early 1960s, private Japanese experts on banks and finance conceived the idea of an Asian development bank, similar to the World Bank, but with focus on Asia (Watanabe 1977, 1–25; Sudo 1992, 54–74). The Japanese government was at first hesitant, but contributing to Asian development through a regional bank gradually became the cornerstone of its economic policy. It supported with enthusiasm the establishment of an Asian development bank, but it was careful enough not to surface as the main advocate of it. When representatives from Asian and developed countries outside of the region finally met in Bangkok from 2 October to 1 November 1965 to lay the foundation of the Asian Development Bank (ADB), the Japanese representative openly and strongly offered Tokyo as the site of the bank's headquarters. By the end of November, eight representatives had offered their own cities: Bangkok, Colombo, Kabul, Kuala Lumpur, Manila, Singapore, Teheran, and Tokyo (Watanabe 1977, 16). A process of secret voting was held, and in the final vote, the Philippines won over Tokyo by one vote (ibid., 17). It was not a total defeat for Japan, however, because Watanabe Takeshi was nominated for the presidency, unopposed, and became the first president of ADB (ibid., 21–22). Since then, the presidents of ADB have always been Japanese.

The twenty-year reparations period officially ended on 22 July 1976. The Treaty of Amity, Commerce and navigation was "ratified" in 1973. ADB firmed up policies and operations in the 1970s. The softly launched cultural policy made slow, uncertain progress through the early 1980s. All these happened under martial law, which was officially lifted in 1981, but virtually remained until the ouster of Marcos through the first People Power Revolution in 1986. Expansion of Japanese ODA to the Philippines was a welcome development for the new Aquino administration that had to face the responsibility of carrying out economic and administrative reforms, including payment of huge foreign debts incurred by the previous administration. The Aquino presidency (February 1986 to May 1992) marked the emergence of Japan as the Philippines' largest source of ODA.

A large portion of Japanese aid to the Philippines consists of loans, which are both bilateral and multilateral. Bilateral loans are easy to understand, but multilateral loans are a bit complicated. ADB is just one of the institutions through which multilateral loans are extended to the Philippines, but its being Asian and located in the Philippines makes it a special bank for the Philippines. And yet, despite its being a part of Metro Manila's landscape since it opened its temporary office in Makati on 19 December 1966 (Watanabe 1977, 47), no major book on Philippines-Japan relations has paid attention to its operations and how it contributes to Philippine development. For this reason, we decided to include a chapter on it (Chapter 6). Written by two insiders, a Japanese and a Filipino, this chapter explains the vision, goals, structure, and operations of ADB. The reader who may ask how the Philippines is faring as a debtor and partner of ADB and what the Philippine government has to do in order to extricate the country from extreme poverty, is invited to read carefully the section on issues and challenges facing the Philippines and Asia in general.

Through the years, Japan has accumulated huge capital through its labor-intensive industrialization. By the start of 1980 Japanese companies had billions for overseas investments (Tecson 2003). Furthermore, because of the high cost of labor brought about by tremendous economic growth, a number of Japanese companies relocated to Southeast Asia in search of cheap labor. The high-speed economic development of Japan was accompanied by a low birth rate and an increase in the number of senior citizens.

The exact opposite was happening in the Philippines: a continuously high birth rate and subsequent increase of employable young people, but there were limited job opportunities to absorb them.

The increase in Japanese investments in the Philippines, the relocation of a number of Japanese companies in the country, and job opportunities in Japan motivated Filipino students to learn the Japanese language and other aspects of Japan. The policy of exporting Filipino labor in order to earn much-needed foreign currency, started in the 1970s, gained momentum, and by the 1980s, Filipinos, mostly female entertainers, were going to Japan by the thousands every year.

The influx of Filipino students and workers to Japan started a cycle of movements of people to and from Japan. Sisters and brothers of Filipino students in Japan also wanted to study in Japan. Sisters, brothers, cousins, and friends of Filipino workers in Japan were also enticed to work in Japan. Filipinos in Japan, regardless of whether they were students, entertainers, unskilled or trained laborers, befriended Japanese. Japanese friends and acquaintances of Filipinos became interested in the Philippines and came to the country to see it for themselves.

It would be a gross exaggeration to say that it is the mighty yen that makes Japan attractive to Filipinos; this would be a big insult to the Filipino women who married their Japanese husbands not because of money but out of love. It would also be an injustice to Filipinos who like things Japanese—cuisine, movies, toys, fashion, arts, and much more—for their admirable qualities.

Love is the third element that defines Philippines-Japan relations. Friendships and acquaintanceships, in a number of cases, have developed into more intimate relationships. Filipino-Japanese marriages numbered more than 7,000 by the mid-1990s (Tokei Joho-bu 2007). Chapter 7, "At the Core of Filipina-Japanese Intercultural Marriages: Family, Gender, Love and Cross-Cultural Understanding," tells us more about interactions between Filipina wives and their Japanese husbands. Chapter 8, on the other hand, tells us the other side of the story: a Filipino husband's adjustment to Japanese culture. While it cannot be denied that the pursuit of higher wages was the motivating factor for Filipina entertainers to work in Japan, neither can it be denied that those who married Japanese men did fall in love. In the case of Filipino recipients of Japanese government scholarships, financial support for higher education is indeed a motivation, but no serious student would apply for such a scholarship if there were no desire to learn about Japan or to study in Japan. It is common knowledge that many Filipinos today, especially the children, teenagers, and young adults, are in love with Japanese *manga* and *anime*. The more classically inclined, although fewer, adore ikebana, Japanese monochrome painting, ceramics, the performing arts, woodblock prints, Japanese cuisine, and other things Japanese. Even if desire was initially created by the lure of financial support, the friendship and collegiality that developed replaces money as the defining characteristic of the relationship. Love, not money, sustains the relationship. Chapter 5, "Networking through the Japan Society for the Promotion of Science," is a personal account of how love of learning, specifically of mathematics, and the desire to develop Filipino mathematics teachers through an exchange program, have resulted in lasting friendships between Japanese and Filipino mathematicians.

THE ELITE AND THE POPULAR

As will be seen in Japan's cultural policy as discussed in Chapter 2, the activities of the Japan Information and Cultural Center described in Chapter 3, the story of the creation of the first Japanese Studies Program narrated in Chapter 4, and the networking through the Japan Society for the Promotion of Science reviewed in Chapter 5, the Japanese government promoted Japanese culture that catered mainly to the elite: the cultural and intellectual elite, as well as the rich. This was especially true before the 1980s. It was only in recent years that the Japan Foundation began to include popular culture, specifically, manga and anime, in its repertoire of activities.

But it was really in the 1980s, with the increase in the volume of movement of peoples to and from the Philippines and Japan, that Japanese popular culture began to spread and reach the greater mass of Filipinos.

Cultural exchanges between the Philippines and Japan are no longer largely defined by the state's cultural policy and programs. What the Japanese government desires to project is now mixed with what the commercialized Japanese goods, mass media, Filipino overseas workers present and accept as Japanese. Chapters 9 and 10, on Filipino films and telenovelas, analyze the projection of the Japanese by Filipinos. Chapter 11, "The Role of Japanese NGOs in Philippines-Japan Relations," on the other hand, presents cultural exchanges between Japanese NGOs and the Filipino poor. It discusses the images formed and the cultural traits learned by both Filipinos and Japanese who interact within the framework of Japanese NGOs. And last but not least, the two chapters on Japanese-Filipino intercultural marriages give us a glimpse of who gets influenced by whom.

MILESTONES, STEPPINGSTONES, AND TURNING POINTS

In eleven chapters, we look into the intricacies of Philippines-Japan relations since the end of the Second World War. Instead of examining each and every event of the bilateral relationship, we present these chapters as samples of the other significant aspects (aside from the economic) of the bilateral relationship.

To link the eleven chapters, and to give space to important events that are not covered in the chapters, we provide a chronology of milestones, steppingstones, and turning points. But even this chronology is selective and contains only important events that led to significant developments and turning points which marked key events or important policy decisions.

The chronology may be read continuously from the first event to the last. Alternatively, the reader may choose to read only the milestones by choosing those with asterisks (*), or the turning points by choosing those marked with intertwined letters S (§), or the steppingstones by choosing those marked with a cross (†). Those which are not marked represent slips or blunders that marred the relationship. This classification is not meant to be taken as conclusive, but rather, as an invitation to the readers to think about it and make their own judgment.

Note

* For an annotated bibliography of English sources from 1935 to 1956, see Ricardo Jose and Lydia Yu Jose 1998.

References

Dela Cruz, Rolando S., ed. 1997. *Image and Reality: Philippines-Japan Relations Towards the 21st Century*. Quezon City: Institute of International Legal Studies, University of the Philippines Law Center.

Embassy of the Philippines in Japan. 1998. *A Friendship of Two Suns.* Tokyo: Embassy of the Philippines in Japan.

Goodman, Grant K. 1967a. Davao: A Case Study in Japanese-Philippine Relations. Kansas: Center for East Asian Studies, University of Kansas.

Goodman, Grant K. 1967b. *Four Aspects of Philippine-Japanese Relations, 1930–1940.* Ann Arbor: Southeast Asian Studies, Yale University.

Ikehata Setsuho and Lydia N. Yu Jose, eds. 2003. *Philippines-Japan Relations.* Quezon City: Ateneo de Manila University Press.

Ikehata Setsuho and Ricardo Trota Jose, eds. 1999. *The Philippines Under Japan.* Quezon City: Ateneo de Manila University Press.

Jose, Lydia N. Yu. 1999. Rev. ed. *Japan Views the Philippines, 1900–1944.* Quezon City: Ateneo de Manila University Press.

_______. 2003. "State and Non-State Actors in Philippines-Japan Relations." *Philippine Studies* 51(2): 177–216.

_______. 2004. "The Japanese Occupation, Nationalism, Textbooks, and Teachers." *The Loyola Schools Review* 3: 159–78.

_______. 2005. "The Japanese Occupation of the Philippines: State and Non-State Memories." *The Journal of Asia-Pacific Studies*, 8: 97–113.

Jose, Lydia N. Yu, and Ricardo Trota Jose. 1998. *An Annotated Bibliography on Philippines-Japan Relations, 1935– 1956.* Manila: Yuchengco Institute of East Asia.

Jose, Ricardo Trota, and Lydia N. Yu Jose. 1997. *Japanese Occupation of the Philippines*, a Pictorial History. Makati City: Ayala Foundation.

Ohno Takushi. 1986. *War Reparations and Peace Settlement: Philippines-Japan Relations, 1945– 1956.* Manila: Solidaridad Publishing House.

Saniel, Josefa. 1969. *Japan and the Philippines, 1868– 1898.* Quezon City: University of the Philippines.

Sato Torao. 1994. *Firipin to Nihon: Koryu 500 nen* [Five Centuries of Filipino-Japanese Relations]. Tokyo: The Simul Press.

Sudo Sueo. 1992. *The Fukuda Doctrine and ASEAN.* Singapore: Institute of Southeast Asian Studies.

Tecson, Gwendolyn R. 2003. "Postwar Japanese Direct Investments." In *Philippines-Japan Relations,* ed. Ikehata Setsuho and Lydia N. Yu Jose, 443–83. Quezon City: Ateneo de Manila University Press.

Tokei Joho-bu [Statistical Information Office]. 2005. *Heisei 17-nen jinko jotai tokei* [Population Survey 2005].Tokyo: Ministry of Labor and Health.

Watanabe Takeshi. 1977. *Towards a New Asia.* Manila: Information Office, Asian Development Bank

Yoshikawa Yoko.1991. *Nippi baisho gaiko kosho no kenkyu, 1949–1956* [War Reparations Negotiations between Japan and the Philippines, 1949– 1956]. Tokyo: Keiso Shobo.

Yoshikawa Yoko. 2003. "War Reparations Implementation, Reparations-Secured Loans and a Treaty of Commerce." In *Philippines-Japan Relations,* ed. Ikehata Setsuho and Lydia N. Yu Jose, 377–442. Quezon City: Ateneo de Manila University Press.

Chapter 1

War Memorials and Commemorations in the Philippines: An Exploratory Look

Ricardo Trota Jose

The end of the Second World War in the Philippines in September 1945 brought to a close three years of trauma in the country. The Philippine government estimated that a total of 1.1 million Filipino lives were lost during the war. Despite the losses suffered, the end of the war brought euphoria over liberation from Japanese domination. The euphoria was short-lived, however, as an avalanche of problems beset the country: court cases against those who had collaborated with the Japanese; working for the recognition of Filipino veterans and the payment of their back pay; reconstructing destroyed and damaged infrastructure, and rehabilitating the country's economy. The Philippines turned to the United States, its wartime ally, for assistance; Japanese were deported from Philippine shores. Memorials for events related to the war were built, and anniversary commemorations were held to remember the wartime events and build up on the partnership between the two wartime allies. As the years passed, however, the tone and emphasis of these memorials and commemorations would change, depending on government priorities and relations with the former allies or the former enemy, Japan.

INTRODUCTION

During the Japanese occupation, memorials and commemorations of wartime events were held, sponsored by the Japanese military. The Fall of Bataan was celebrated in 1943 and 1944, not as a day of defeat and as a way of remembering the Filipino veterans, but as a Japanese victory. These took place within just one year—1943—after the surrender in Bataan, and few Filipinos felt sympathy with the Japanese. There was no mention of the Death March and Filipino heroism, and it was a hollow celebration, since the pain of the suffering was still very real (*Tribune* 1943, 1944; Lichauco 1949). The Japanese built their own memorials in Bataan and Corregidor to commemorate the heroism of their own war dead. One memorial to the Filipino defenders of Bataan and Corregidor, however, was built in 1942 and still exists to this day: a memorial to Filipinos who died in Capas during the months when they were concentrated in Camp O'Donnell. The Japanese camp authorities allowed the Filipino prisoners of war to build the simple memorial, which was formally inaugurated in November 1942.

At the end of the war Filipinos saw the war as something worth remembering, commemorating and being proud of. The Philippines was, after all, a member of the Allied Powers and was one of the victors. Despite the defeat at Bataan and Corregidor, which were perceived as gallant fighting defeats, there were also days of victory, and other days which were historically significant. Among these were the day the war began (8 December 1941), the day the Japanese took Manila (2 January 1942), the fall of Bataan (9 April 1942) and the fall of Corregidor (6 May 1942). These days were engraved in the memories of the Filipino people. Individual towns and cities recalled the time when they were occupied by the Japanese . There were organization days for the various guerrilla resistance groups, the days of the first US air raids on the Philippines, and then the days of liberation for the different towns and cities. Some of these days would become days of commemoration—officially or unofficially—and would be occasions for remembering the war. To help perpetuate the memory of certain incidents, individuals, or guerrilla units, memorials and historical markers were put up, either by the Philippine government or by private Filipino groups. Some places had become well known during the war: Bataan, Corregidor, Leyte, Lingayen, as well as several battle sites throughout the country, and it was here that some of the early markers were built.

Americans, on the other hand, remembered a bit differently. American veterans commemorated the campaigns they had fought. The US government recognized its men and women who had fallen in battle and tried to build on the US-Philippine alliance during the war. There were memorials put up by military units to record their victories and remember their dead; the US government put up temporary military cemeteries with a view to building a proper battle memorial in the future.

The Japanese, on the other hand, although defeated, looked on the war as a holy war. For them, commemorating the war in the Philippines had more than just historical and political value; it had a spiritual aspect. This explains why many of the Japanese memorials have a Buddhist or Shinto character, and why commemorations involve religious ceremonies. Furthermore, almost half a million Japanese died in the Philippines during the war, the largest number of war dead in one country in Southeast Asia and the Pacific. Due to the wounds inflicted on Filipinos during the war, however, the Japanese recognized that it would not be politically correct to bring in their own views of the war unless they were apologies, atonements, or statements about friendly relations in the future. But it would take time before the Japanese could return to the Philippines, since Filipino memories of Japan were very negative for many years.

The Early Years after the War: 1945–1950

The first official commemorations and memorials in the Philippines were those of US Army units shortly after the fighting. Examples are the 33rd Infantry Division's memorials in Baguio; this division fought stiff Japanese resistance to get to the city. Balete Pass was renamed Dalton Pass after Brig. Gen. James L. Dalton II, killed in the fighting, and a marker was placed at the top of the pass in his, and his division's memory. (The Philippine Congress made the name official.) The only Mexican fighter squadron to fight outside Mexico fought in the Philippines in 1945, and lost some pilots. At the end of the war they, too, put up a memorial which still stands just outside Intramuros. Some of the other early memorials still exist, but the commemorations and memorials were held basically for the unit concerned, for posterity, unit pride, and for remembering those who died in combat. "We shall not forget" is one theme which was common to these memorials and commemorations, a theme which still underlies many American memorials and ceremonies in the Philippines today. The memorials depicted glory—nationalism, patriotism, bravery; and loss, usually depicted as a glorious loss.[1]

Philippine memorials and commemorations would follow similar lines. The Philippines became independent in 1946, and the government faced immense challenges to rebuild after the war. But the national government realized the need to pay tribute to the war dead and to the veterans who had fought for freedom. There were several war cemeteries around the country, but the most important of them—in the sense that it had the largest number of dead—was the cemetery of the former prisoners-of-war camp at Camp O'Donnell, in Capas, Tarlac. The first official memorial ceremonies, on 30 November 1946 and 1947, marked by speeches by President Manuel Roxas and Vice President Elpidio Quirino, respectively, were held on the camp grounds (Roxas 1954, 274). The date was National Heroes Day, a national holiday commemorated before the war honoring Filipino heroes from all periods of Philippine history. The choice of the site was significant, and so were the speeches, which recognized and thanked the dead soldiers, and promised to continue the task of building the nation. The speeches expressed the political theme of these and subsequent ceremonies.

There were other cemeteries for the Second World War dead, most being makeshift, in Manila, in Bataan, in Fort Santiago (which had been the Kempeitai headquarters and site of massacres at the end of the war), and in Manila's North Cemetery, where the Kempeitai had executed many victims.

Many battle sites were still dangerous right after the war, or were difficult to reach because of the nature of the roads and lack of transportation. The island fortress of Corregidor was still littered with unexploded ordnance, and its position was so strategic that it would remain in US hands until 1947, when the "Rock" was formally turned over to the Philippine government. Both Roxas and Quirino spoke at the turnover ceremony, emphasizing the importance of working for peace and highlighting the US-Philippine partnership. The island henceforth became a pilgrimage site for Filipinos and Americans. (Quirino 1955, 67–69; Roxas 1954, 532). Themes which would be repeated in many of the speeches of this period up until the 1950s were: the importance of working for peace, remembering the valiant deeds of the Filipino and American comrades-in-arms, and maintaining a vibrant US-Philippines relationship.

These themes were echoed in the early historical markers put up by the Philippine Historical Committee. In Bataan, an early marker read: "The little mountainous peninsula of Bataan saved democracy and the whole world from the evil hands of the devil" (National Historical Institute 1993, 336). The marker still stands, in an enclosed area in the town of Hermosa. Bataan and Corregidor, for which Filipinos fought beyond human endurance, became the main symbols of the war in the Philippines. Anger against Japan still seethed and would not abate until more than ten years later.

The Philippine Historical Commission (now known as the National Historical Institute), the government agency tasked to put up official historical markers, also quickly put up markers in Palo, Leyte, where General MacArthur and then-Commonwealth President of the Philippines Sergio Osmeña, landed in October 1944. Next to Bataan and Corregidor, Leyte would be the next most important place in the commemorations of the Second World War. Other significant sites where official markers were installed were Lingayen, where the US forces landed in 1945 to commence the liberation of Luzon from the Japanese; and the US High Commissioner's residence in Baguio, where General Yamashita signed the surrender documents on 3 September 1945 (National Historical Institute 1993).

In addition to the Philippine Historical Committee, local governments and private groups—particularly veterans groups—put up their own memorials and markers to commemorate their own battles, martyrs, or, in some instances, tragedies. Various towns and cities celebrated their own days of liberation and continue to do so today. For example, Mandaluyong commemorates its liberation every year on 13 February, which is also the same date when the town became a city.

Organized partly to perpetuate the memories of the war were various veterans' groups. Most guerrilla organizations had their own associations. As there were so many groups, it became necessary to organize a federation, and in 1946 a Confederation of Legions of Philippine Veterans was organized which held national conventions. The Confederation was important enough for the Philippine president to give the keynote speech. These various associations participated in early commemorations of liberation and independence days, but a major reason for their creation was to fight for veterans' rights and benefits. Many of them extolled relations with the US; in fact, there are a number of US veterans' organizations—such as the American Legion and the Veterans of Foreign Wars—still in the Philippines. Ties with the US at this time were particularly strong, especially with the start of the Cold War. In the late 1940s these veterans were young, and many were starting their careers in politics and business.[2]

THE 1950S: TEN YEARS AFTER THE ONSET OF THE WAR

By 1951, some time had passed since the war, but war memories were still very vivid, and events that took place during the Second World

War were common knowledge. However, the Cold War had grown more tense with the advent of a nuclear showdown: the Communist threat to the government was very real, and veterans were actively involved in government, business, and diplomacy. The Hukbalahap war veterans, being on the Communist side and openly challenging the government, were of course left out of all ceremonies.

Commemorations of war-related events became more institutionalized, with the fall of Bataan becoming a national holiday through presidential proclamation. The President himself attended official programs close to or in places where battles had taken place. President Ramon Magsaysay, for example, attended the first Bataan Day held in Balanga, Bataan, with many defenders present. Bataan Day became a symbol of the war, and speeches extolled the heroism of both Filipinos and Americans, at a time when the Fil-American relationship was considered a "special relationship."

One reason for the institutionalization of war-related days and sites was that specific veterans groups, such as the Defenders of Bataan and Corregidor (DBC), were organized not only to fight for veterans' benefits but also to make the veterans useful citizens of the country, as well as to keep the memory of their sacrifices alive (Defenders of Bataan and Corregidor 1956, 13–16).

Since the 1950s saw the worsening of the Cold War, the US-Philippine alliance in the Second World War played a more significant role in the commemorations of the decade. Many of the veterans were in their prime and were called upon to contribute to the security of the country.

But the 1950s also saw a rise of nationalism in the Philippines, accompanied particularly by dissatisfaction arising from the presence of US bases on Philippine soil, unbalanced trade relations between the US and the Philippines, and the festering veterans' recognition issue. The US Congress had denied many Filipino veterans their benefits and recognition, and relations between the US and the Philippines would become officially colder, as interests clashed. Many Filipinos, however, remained overwhelmingly pro-American.

At this time, the Japanese were not invited to these war commemorations, since memories of the war were still vivid and a strong sense of antagonism against Japan remained. The Philippines and Japan had not yet normalized relations, since the reparations agreement was still being hammered out.

In 1956, the reparations agreement with Japan was ratified, reopening formal relations between the two countries. Although the public perception of Japan was very negative and angry, the government allowed a Japanese group to come to the Philippines in 1958 to gather the bones of Japanese war dead (Nakano 2003, 343–47). The reception they met was still angry, for although some Filipinos were willing to forgive, they could not forget. In order not to offend the Filipinos, the Japanese stated that they would also recognize the "heroic spirits of Filipino civilians and military with all due respect" in their prayers and rituals. Since the rituals were conducted in Japanese, however, there was no way of verifying whether this was true. The rituals were basically Buddhist, as the Japanese bone-recovering missions were not simply meant to reinter the dead, but to appease their souls. In any case, this group stayed away from media.

A constant reminder of the war was the presence of Japanese stragglers, who were still fairly numerous in the mountains in the 1950s. There were also physical signs of the war: the ruins of Intramuros would remain largely untouched until the 1970s, and bombs and other war relics were plentiful.

The 1960s: Twentieth and Twenty-fifth Anniversaries

The start of the 1960s saw the Philippine government trying out more nationalistic policies as opposed to the strong pro-American stand just after the war. General MacArthur, then in retirement, was sent by the US government on an official sentimental voyage to the Philippines in 1961, which rekindled the euphoria for a while (I Shall Return 1961; Sentimental Journey 1961).

Twentieth-anniversary ceremonies were held for Bataan, Corregidor, Leyte and a few other locations. Markers were put up by the newly organized Veterans Federation of the Philippines, and the sprawling Manila American Cemetery—the largest outside the US—was completed in Fort Bonifacio (formerly Fort William McKinley) and opened to the public (American Battle Monuments Commission 1976, 4–7).[3] The Philippine government also put up a state cemetery (Libingan ng mga Bayani) near the US cemetery, the bulk of those initially buried being the war dead from Camp O'Donnell.

While US-Philippine ties were still emphasized, times were changing, and the ship which took MacArthur around during his visit was made in Japan, part of Japanese reparations. The Philippines was slowly reopening to Japan. A year after MacArthur's visit, the Japanese crown prince also visited the Philippines, to a warm albeit at first distanced welcome. From a distance of twenty years, many people were able to distinguish the newer generation in Japan from the wartime generation, although rancor still remained.

The twenty-fifth anniversary commemorations were major events covered not only locally but also throughout the world. Philippine President Ferdinand Marcos, himself a war veteran who had fought in Bataan, had been incarcerated in prison camp, and joined the guerrillas. His political campaign capitalized on his heroism during the war, and he was an honored guest at veterans' conventions.[4] To commemorate the twenty-fifth anniversary of the Second World War in the Philippines, plans were made for a grand series of ceremonies in Manila, in Bataan and elsewhere, from 1967 to 1970. Reunions of veterans were set. Construction of a massive cross on top of Mount Samat—a mountain which was key for control of the peninsula where much fighting had taken place—was started. The cornerstone was laid in 1966, and the main memorial ceremonies were held at its site in 1967. Due to lack of funds, however, its completion was delayed; the Dambana ng Kagitingan (Altar of Valor) was finally inaugurated formally in 1970. Individual kilometer posts marking every single kilometer of the Death March were inaugurated. For the first time, the

Japanese ambassador was invited, although he was given no speaking part (25th Bataan Day Program 1967; *Life* 1967, 6–9).

The speeches and messages of the Twenty-fifth Anniversary of Bataan harkened back to Fil-American friendship, the need to fight for freedom, as well as the importance of remembering the sacrifices of Filipinos and Americans. But Marcos also brought in the present, and the need to continue the fight—against poverty, ignorance and disease. It was a political speech, and conspicuously, he did not mention Japan.

The Twenty-fifth Anniversary of the Fall of Corregidor was also marked by lavish ceremonies, as the Americans began construction of the Pacific War Memorial, to commemorate not only the war in the Philippines but also other battles in the Pacific.[5]

Twenty-fifth anniversaries of the US landing at Leyte in 1944, of the Battle of Bessang Pass in North Luzon, of the entry of American troops into Manila, and of the liberation of certain towns and cities on specific dates were also commemorated. Many cities and towns put up memorials to remind people of the travails of war or to honor Filipino veterans. Many of these memorials included relics of the war: a tourist attraction in Zamboanga City is the "Gun of Aggression"—two Japanese guns placed in a rotunda. Smaller towns exhibit Japanese helmets, machine guns or small artillery pieces. (Two guns in front of the General Headquarters building of the Armed Forces of the Philippines in Camp Aguinaldo are, interestingly, Japanese guns, with no marker).

A unique group is the War Heroes Committee of Ateneo de Manila University, which put a memorial in the university to honor its alumni who saw action in the Second World War and other historical events. Installed in December 1969, it is the only one of its type in any school in the Philippines and has been expanded to contain a small museum. Names continue to be added to those honored (Ateneo de Manila University Heroes Hall Directory 2002).

In contrast with the close US-Philippine ties which were emphasized in the formal ceremonies, dissent and anti-US sentiment were prevalent in universities, labor groups and sectors of media at this time due to the Vietnam War, unequal trade relations, the difficulty of getting recognition for veterans, and protests that the Philippines was a victim of neocolonialism. This led some Filipinos to question the commemoration of the Second World War itself, since activists viewed it as an imperialist war. The government and the veterans fought back, defending their heritage.[6]

The Martial Law Years

Marcos declared martial law in 1972 and remained in power until 1986. During those fourteen years, war commemorations received much attention and many memorials were built by the government. The fact that Marcos was a veteran—supposedly the most decorated Filipino war hero—gave veterans' affairs a prominent place during this period, particularly since many war veterans occupied key positions in government and in the military.[7]

Regular official commemorations were held at Bataan, Corregidor, Leyte and Bessang Pass, while towns and cities held their own commemorations. These typically consisted of wreath-laying, speeches praising the heroes of the war, announcing new veterans' benefits. In the case of Leyte, the ceremonies usually involved a reenactment of the American landing, with the highlight being an actor playing MacArthur wading ashore and proclaiming that he had returned. In these reenactments, US and Philippine armed forces worked hand in hand, just as they had in 1944. The commemorations also became venues for the announcement of government policies; as time went on, the speeches focused more on government policies while the historical content diminished. Marcos's speeches on these occasions also shifted from close US relations towards greater self-reliance, and opened up towards Japan.

In 1975, a memorial shrine was put up in Kiangan, the Bantayog sa Kiangan (Kiangan Shrine). This shrine was unique because it used native architecture as its motif, memorializing the mountain peoples who fought in the guerrilla resistance. Kiangan was significant as the place where General Yamashita surrendered to the American forces in 1945. Although Mt. Samat and Kiangan are called shrines, they do not have the religious significance of the Japanese memorials.

While the National Historical Institute and other Filipino and American groups continued to put up their own memorials or markers, the 1970s would see more Japanese memorials constructed. Although Marcos kept close ties with the US, he opened up to Japan. The President, in the first year of martial law, unilaterally ratified the Treaty of Amity, Commerce and Navigation between the Philippines and Japan, which had been the subject of debates in the Philippine Congress for over a decade. With its ratification, the doors to Japanese trade and investment were opened. The Philippines invited Japanese businessmen, as well as Japanese veterans, to come to the country.

Since the Americans and Filipinos had their own war cemeteries, Marcos allowed the Japanese to construct a memorial to the Japanese war dead at Caliraya, in Laguna. This was the first large-scale war memorial built by the Japanese government outside Japan; it was formally turned over to the Philippine government in 1976. Caliraya would become a center of Japanese pilgrimages apart from specific battlefields (Nakano 2003, 337–76; Ishida 2001, 266–74).

The Japanese began sending organized groups to the Philippines, to visit former battle sites, collect the remains of the war dead, and put up their own memorials. Unit memorials mushroomed throughout the Philippines, starting in 1973, from small wooden strips to large towers. Some inscriptions were written in Japanese, others in Japanese and Tagalog, others in Japanese, English, and Tagalog. The Japanese text was almost always the same, praying for the repose of Japanese souls. Some of the markers included the names of Filipinos and Americans, and almost all appealed for peace. In a number of cases, however, the Japanese text did not correspond with the English or Tagalog text; some Japanese memorials expressed repentance for the death and destruction caused by the war, while others only mentioned the Japanese. The memorials were put up by veterans' groups, local governments, private groups such as the Japanese Lions Club, and so on. Most of these memorials are in battlefields, but a few are in cemeteries, such as Muntinlupa Prison, where some Japanese war criminals were executed, and in Los Baños, marking the place of execution of Generals Homma Masaharu and Yamashita Tomoyuki.[8]

Not all Japanese memorials were put up by Japanese. In the 1970s there existed in Angeles, Pampanga, the Kamikaze Memorial Society (Kameso), dedicated to the memory of the Kamikaze pilots. By 1975 the society had put up a marker at the location of the airfield from which the first Kamikaze mission took off. Another marker was placed on the house where the Kamikaze idea was first broached by Admiral Ohnishi Takijiro. These markers attracted Japanese tourists and put the area on the tourist map (*Bulletin Today* 1975, 1).[9]

The Japanese memorials were different from the Filipino and American memorials in that they were also religious shrines and not just historical in nature. Visiting Japanese brought gifts for Filipinos where the memorials were erected, and tried to get them to maintain the memorials. Filipinos regarded some memorials as tourist attractions but for most the significance of the memorials declined as years passed. Few Filipinos understood the religious significance of these memorials. A resident of Lipa, Batangas, told a Japanese writer: "I don't have much interest in it [Japanese memorial services]. They just come and go in our town and we just look at them" (Ishida 2001, 254–66).

Japanese Prime Minister Nakasone Yasuhiro visited the Philippines and is reported to have said that he felt very welcome in the Philippines. What is significant is that Nakasone had been stationed in Davao as a junior naval officer during the war but was not criticized for this (Nakano 2003, 340–41).

The erection of the Caliraya memorial and the other Japanese memorials attracted Japanese tours to these spots, linking them to the government's ongoing program to attract tourists to visit the Philippines. The Marcos administration made tourism a big program, and in 1977 the President announced a Reunion for Peace to which all veterans of the Second World War were invited. It would be an opportunity to showcase the gains of the Philippines under martial law and boost tourism as well, while fostering friendship among former allies and enemies. Americans, Japanese, Australians—anyone who had fought in the Philippines during the war was invited to a reunion of former warriors (Marcos 1975; Department of Tourism 1977).

Bataan Day 1977—the thirty-fifth anniversary of the surrender—was unique in that the ceremonies saw the participation of Filipinos, Americans, and Japanese. Previous celebrations had excluded the Japanese; this time three groups of buses gathered at the top of Mount Samat and all three groups participated in the commemorative ceremonies. There was some tension, and the Japanese group remained apart from the American and Filipino veterans.[10]

Other commemorations in 1977 were lavish, government-sponsored affairs; the one in Leyte was participated in by Americans, Filipinos, Japanese, Australians and others who were involved in the battles for the island. The landing was reenacted full-scale, and formal ceremonies were held near the larger-than-life statues of General MacArthur, President Osmeña, and their landing party. Of course, it helped that Marcos's wife, Imelda, was from Leyte.

The Japanese war tours peaked in 1977, because aside from the Reunion for Peace program, it was the thirty-third year after the battle—a significant year in the Buddhist calendar (Nakano 2003, 365).

Anti-American sentiment continued during martial law. The question of why the Philippines celebrated defeats came up again. Apparently in response to this, Marcos first changed the name Bataan Day to Araw ng Kagitingan (Day of Valor). Since the criticisms continued, Marcos moved the Day of Valor from Bataan Day (9 April) to Corregidor Day (6 May) in 1979. Although the fall of Corregidor was another defeat, it occurred between the fall of Bataan and the victory at Bessang Pass (14 June). Bessang Pass, aside from being a significant guerrilla victory, was also supposedly where Marcos won a number of his medals. Bataan Day, a national holiday since the 1950s, ceased to be a holiday.

The first commemoration of Araw ng Kagitingan on 6 May 1980 was held at Fort Santiago, where the Kempeitai had their headquarters during the war. Marcos's speech dealt less with history and memory and more with current national policies, particularly with the government's sentiments against war and its policy of keeping Philippine territorial sovereignty sacred. Wreaths were laid by the American and Japanese ambassadors; US Ambassador Richard W. Murphy paid tribute to Filipino nationalism, which, he said, was needed to make the Philippines strong. He also stated that while special relations between the US and the Philippines had ended, both now maintained a relationship of mutual trust and confidence. These speeches were considerably different from those delivered a few years earlier; they also reflected the recent US policy of averting a third world war with the help of allies. Japanese ambassador Tanaka Hideho announced that the world seemed to be in turmoil and "we must renew our resolve not to create a situation which may develop into another war." As for Japan itself: "we shall never cause war in the future" (*Daily Express* 1980, 1, 6).

Becoming, in a sense, an artificial holiday, it did not strike the veterans' groups or the public at large as very significant, since the rationale for Araw ng Kagitingan was not clear and focused. In fact, despite the official government celebration of Araw ng Kagitingan on 6 May, veterans groups would still observe Bataan Day and Bessang Pass Day separately.

Other major war commemorations were held from 1982 to 1985, the fortieth anniversary of the war. The ceremonies for Bataan Day 1982 were again big government affairs, involving almost all branches of government and the veterans' organizations. Again, Japanese, Americans, and Filipinos attended major functions, but not everything worked out as planned. At Mount Samat, some Filipino veterans reached out and shook hands with the Japanese while others stayed back; the Americans steered clear of the Japanese. The event's organizers sought to bring all sides together under one roof for lunch, but some American veterans walked out of the venue, refusing to be with the Japanese. Despite the lapse of forty years, animosity was still there.

Speeches again told of courage and valor—and US-Philippines ties. Included, however, were references to Philippines-Japan relations and friendship. It was at about this time that Japanese atrocities were apparently played down in some markers, the Japanese text of which omitted any mention of these. As for the veterans, the government speeches made scant reference to their honor and the benefits due them, and laid more stress on what role the veterans could play in building the so-called New Society.

The Leyte commemoration in 1984 was another big affair, with commemorative stamps, exhibits and a reenactment of the US landing with US and Philippine armed forces. Both armed forces exhibited their prowess, and, as with previous commemorations, the event was seen as an opportunity to advertise the gains Leyte had made in industry, tourism, and other fields. It was also tied up with the groundbreaking ceremonies at the National Maritime Polytechnic Complex, financed by Japan. Markers were installed, joint US-Japan-Philippines programs were held, but the arrival hours of the guests were so timed that they would not be in the airport at the same time (Leyte Provincial Government 1984).

War memories would, by this time, be clouded by cynicism and disappointment. The exposure of corruption and cronyism in Marcos's administration, as well as human rights abuses, dealt serious blows to the President. These issues, topped by charges that Marcos's medals were fake, tainted the Second World War commemorations, which were seen as part of an administration that was crumbling.[11] The younger generation, which had not experienced the war first-hand, looked with suspicion and disbelief at some of the commemorations, also criticizing them as a waste of money and a sign of colonial mentality. With Japan as a major economic partner, and Japanese foreign investments pouring in, some Filipinos began to say openly that it was unwise to bring out stories of Japanese atrocities.

Looking Back, Moving Further: From 1986 to the Fiftieth Anniversary

The downfall of Marcos brought in President Cory Aquino, the daughter-in-law of a prominent wartime collaborationist, Benigno Aquino Sr., although the younger generation was unaware of this. Despite this, and a seeming bias favoring Japan which was expected to assist the Philippines, Aquino did more for the veterans and some Second World War commemorations than Marcos did during his last years in power.

In 1986, shortly after she took office, Aquino directed the Department of Tourism to develop Corregidor into a war memorial and tourist destination. The Corregidor Foundation, Inc. was created to oversee this task, which included upgrading facilities, putting up a light-and-sound presentation in Malinta Tunnel, cleaning up tourist spots, constructing a Filipino War Memorial and marketing the island better. It was expected to be ready by 1992, the fiftieth anniversary of the island's fall to the Japanese. A Japanese memorial would also be set up, but it would be segregated and located where the Japanese dead had been buried right after the battle. Corregidor was dubbed the Island of Valor, Peace, and International Understanding, and became a popular tourist destination (Philippine Information Agency 1991; Department of Tourism 1990).

Aquino restored Araw ng Kagitingan to 9 April, a day more meaningful to the veterans and the people. In order to dampen criticism of the Filipino penchant for commemorating defeats, she expanded the commemorative period to one week and designated it as Veterans Week in order to honor veterans of all the Philippine wars.

As the nation was in a critical state at this time—with a crippled economy, serious social inequality and the threat of coups—Aquino's speeches in the memorial ceremonies called for modern-day heroes to stand up to oppression, but also appealed for greater recognition of the veterans (Aquino 1989; *Bulletin Today* 1990a).

Because of the coup attempts and perceived political instability, the number of veterans' groups coming from Japan decreased, particularly after a high-profile case in which a Japanese businessman was kidnapped. The number of American veterans who came to the Philippines decreased, too, as they grew older and found it difficult to travel. The commemorations thus became more Filipino-oriented, unlike the big international affairs they were in the 1970s and early 1980s.

Aquino needed support from Japan and made two state visits to Japan. The Emperor allegedly apologized to her very profusely for the war, but this report was denied by the official Malacañang spokesmen. Japan was increasingly important to the Filipinos; numerous Filipinos were going to Japan to find work. Thus, there would be little government criticism of Japan's conduct during the war, Japanese textbooks that glossed over Japanese atrocities, the existence of "comfort women," and the Yasukuni Shrine (Nakano 2003, 338–39).

Even if there was no outright criticism of Japan, various groups commemorated the Death March—from boy scouts, to historians, to concerned Japanese professors and their students (who called it a March for Life) (*Bulletin Today* 1990a, 1; 1990b, 1).

Although Aquino may not have wanted to confront the Japanese with their wartime atrocities, she could not escape the fact that she would have to face the fiftieth anniversary of the Second World War. She issued a proclamation which declared 8 December 1991 to 8 December 1992 as a commemorative period for the observation of the fiftieth anniversary of the war in the Philippines. The theme adopted was: Kagitingan, Kapayapaan, Kaunawaan—Valor, Peace and Understanding (Aquino 1991).

The commemorative year started with a formal ceremony at Malacañang Palace on 8 December 1991. Aquino's speech was a pledge to promote international understanding. She also emphasized the steps needed to give the veterans more benefits (Defenders of Bataan and Corregidor 1992, 4–6). Close ties with the US were barely mentioned, because the US bases treaty had just been terminated by the Philippine Senate, thus causing a rift between the US and the Philippines. In the same ceremony, the Japanese ambassador (Goto Toshio) expressed "deep remorse" for the Second World War (*Philippine Daily Inquirer* 1991).

The 1992 Veterans Week was typical of previous commemorations but was more subdued and overshadowed by political developments and the forthcoming presidential election.

Fidel V. Ramos succeeded Aquino as president, and under him the country would formally observe the fiftieth anniversary of the liberation of the Philippines and the end of the war. Ramos being a former military officer and a veteran (albeit of the Korean War), he pushed for big commemorations of the fiftieth anniversary. His speeches, however, departed still further from the historical events and sounded more like policy statements or state-of-the-nation addresses. His Bataan Day 1993 speech, for example, focused on the fight against poverty, national stagnation, corruption, divisiveness, and environmental degradation, with Filipinos being called on to show heroism. Not just the heroism of 1942, but also the heroism of 1996 (*DBC Newsletter* 1993, 13–14).

Despite all these activities, the official ceremonies neglected one sector: the civilians who died during the war. In the 1990s, an organization called Memorare Manila 1945 was formed, a civilian association of survivors of the battle of Manila. The aim of this group was "to honor the victims by keeping alive their memory, by collecting eyewitness accounts and depositing them in archives, by encouraging the publication of books and articles regarding the liberation of Manila, by encouraging the creation of similar societies elsewhere in the country and, by putting up appropriate memorials whenever and wherever possible" (Perez de Olaguer 2005, i). In February 1995, Memorare Manila 1945 organized several masses to remember the civilian dead, and put up a memorial inside Intramuros, where hundreds had been killed.

On the other hand, another organization, the Filipino-American Memorial Endowment Foundation (FAME), was organized to keep the memory of Philippine-American wartime sacrifice alive. Among their projects was the replacement of the Bataan Death March markers with more permanent markers.

Twenty-first Century: Sixtieth Anniversary

After the turn of the new century, Bataan Day continued to be observed. In 2003, the Capas Shrine was further developed with the opening of a Wall of Heroes on which are inscribed the names of those who fought in Bataan and died in Capas. The official ceremonies, however, dwelt more on the war against terror (this being after 11 September 2001), than the historical significance of the memorial and the actions it memorialized (see Jose 2005, 101–2).

Ironically, while the programs were supposed to honor the veterans, they usually turned into political speeches hardly related to the events being commemorated; speeches were more about Official Development Assistance and other forms of aid. The veterans would usually be left in the hot sun waiting for the VIPs to arrive, and then would await their boxed lunches. Sadly, they would usually be relegated to the background. While the commemoration meant free food and a free trip, it was more trying for the aging veterans.

Despite the number of memorials and markers existing today, there are still many sites and groups not represented. The Comfort Women were only lately remembered with a marker by the City of Manila (in Liwasang Bonifacio) in cooperation with nongovernment organizations assisting the women.

Planning for the sixtieth anniversary commemorations started late, and suffered from failure to consult the right persons or groups. There was initially no initiative from top levels of government, and it seems some push had to come from the US embassy. A joint multi-agency group was formed, but it was late and the choice of events haphazard. Some of the planning was tainted by politics and suffered from lack of funds. Even so, several commemorations have been carried out, either by government or private groups.

Not commemorated, with no marker or memorial, are a number of events in the war. There is nothing commemorating officially the Japanese-sponsored republic under President Jose P. Laurel. Neither is there anything to show where the pro-Japanese groups such as the Makapili were formed or operated. This is understandable since these are things most Filipinos are not proud of; but they are part of history nevertheless.

Where the formal commemorations are quiet, the movies filled some of the void. In the last five years, several war movies were made, dealing with different themes. One, "Yamashita: The Tiger's Treasure," dealt with the story of the alleged treasure, based on the story of one who claims to have seen it. There are other movies which show alternative perceptions of the war and the occupation.

It might be mentioned in closing that there is a big Japanese memorial for the Philippines in Aichi Prefecture (the Hito Kannon), although it is dedicated to the Japanese war dead. There are several veterans' groups in Japan, many of which are conventional, patriotic groups, but there are a few which seek to help impoverished Filipinos and, in an indirect way, attempt to make up for the death and destruction brought about by the Second World War (an example is the Sampagita Kai based in Kyoto).

Sixty years have now passed since the end of the Second World War, and this article has shown how the commemorations and memorials have changed with time. These, while all dealing with the war, vary in content and treatment and in their own way reveal the changing memories of the war. Today, the Japanese ambassador is given a more active role, one which he has taken up. There is still a bit of anger at Japanese participation in some ceremonies, particularly among veterans, but the official government line is one of friendship and cooperation.

Notes

1. Many of the unit histories of the US Army have photographs of their memorials and the commemorative ceremonies. See, for example, Karolevitz (1946, 152).

2. The groups put out souvenir programs and other publications reporting their activities and occasionally, historical accounts of the war. The 6th Military District Veterans Association has been publishing annual programs on the occasion of the liberation of Panay.

3. A total of 17,206 war dead are interred, with the names of an additional 36,282 missing engraved on memorial walls.

4. See the political campaign advertisements, particularly in the *Philippines Free Press*, for Marcos's use of his veteran exploits during the 1965 presidential campaign.

5. For these and subsequent ceremonies, see the various commemorative programs.

6. An example of criticism is Quijano de Manila's "What Really Happened in Bataan," (1963, 36–39; 67), which presented a less glorious version of the campaign. Veterans and the Defenders of Bataan and Corregidor quickly responded in subsequent issues.

7. The author was able to meet many of these veterans and personally attended several of the memorial rites in the 1970s and 1980s.

8. List of Japanese memorials in *Shuroku Ruson* (1988, 2–25). Some more were put up later; some are not in this list. A number have ceased to exist or are difficult to locate now.

9. An earlier group came in 1974, by which time the Kamikaze East airfield marker was already up (*Bulletin Today* 1974, 14).

10. The author attended this and other related ceremonies.

11. In 1982, the small newspaper *We Forum* published a series of articles alleging Marcos's medals were not genuine. Marcos responded by closing the newspaper. The resulting public outcry, however, prevented Marcos from going further and jailing the staff.

References

American Battle Monuments Commission. 1976. *Manila American Cemetery and Memorial.*: Government Printing Office.

Aquino, Corazon C. 1989. Presidential Proclamation 466, signed 14 September.

———. 1991. Proclamation 758, signed 12 July; Memorandum Order 344 s. 1991.

Ateneo de Manila University Heroes Hall Directory, 1969–1999. 2002. Quezon City: Ateneo de Manila University Archives.

Bulletin Today. 1974. "Kamikaze Birthplace Attracts Japanese, American Tourists." 7 August.

Bulletin Today. 1975. "Surviving Kamikaze Men Due Here." 7 March.

———. 1990a. "Fall of Bataan Recalled," "Vets Week Under Way." 9 April.

———. 1990b. "Death March Retraced." 15 April.

Daily Express. 1980. "FM Stresses RP's Policy Against War." 7 May.

DBC Newsletter. 1993. June.

Defenders of Bataan and Corregidor. 1956. Commemorative booklet.

———. 1992. *DBC Golden Anniversary Souvenir Publication*. Quezon City: Defenders of Bataan and Corregidor.

Department of Tourism. 1977. Reunion for Peace brochure. Manila: Department of Tourism.

———. 1990. *Corregidor: Island of Valor, Peace and International Understanding.* Manila: Department of Tourism.

"I Shall Return." 1961. Pamphlet

Ishida Jintaro. 2001. *The Remains of War: Apology and Forgiveness.* Quezon City: Megabooks Company.

Jose, Lydia N. Yu. 2005. "The Japanese Occupation of the Philippines: State and Non-State Memories." *Asia Pacific Studies* 8: 97–113.

Karolevitz, (Captain) Robert F. 1946. *The 25th Division and World War 2.* Baton Rouge: Army and Navy Publishing Company.

Leyte Provincial Government. 1984. *Peace and Progress: 40th Leyte Landing Anniversary*. Tacloban: Leyte Provincial Government.

Lichauco, Marcial P. 1949. *Dear Mother Putnam.* (Privately published.)

Life. 1967. (Asia edition). "Bataan's Solemn 25th Anniversary." 1 May.

Marcos, Ferdinand E. 1975. Letter of Instruction No. 331, signed 29 October (mimeographed).

Nakano Satoshi. 2003. "The Politics of Mourning." In *Philippines-Japan Relations,* ed. Ikehata Setsuho and Lydia N. Yu Jose.. Quezon City: Ateneo de Manila University Press.

National Historical Institute. 1993. *Historical Markers.* 3 vols. Manila: Bureau of Printing.

Perez de Olaguer, Antonio. 2005. (English translation by Trinidad Ongtangco Regala) *Terror in Manila: February 1945.* Manila: Memorare Manila Foundation.

Philippine Daily Inquirer. 1991. 9 December.

Philippine Information Agency. 1991. *Salute to the Retaking of Corregidor Island.* Manila: Philippine Information Agency.

Philippines Free Press. 1965. Various issues.

Quijano de Manila. 1963. "What Really Happened in Bataan." *Philippines Free Press*, 6 April.

Quirino, Elpidio. 1955. *The Quirino Way.* Manila: privately published.

Roxas, Manuel.1954. *Speeches, Addresses and Messages of President Roxas.* Vol. 1. Manila: Bureau of Printing.

Sentimental Journey. 1961. Manila: US Information Service.

Shuroku Ruson. 1988. No. 11, August.

Tribune. 1943. 11, 12 April.

———. 1944 11, 12 April.

25th Bataan Day .1967. Program. Manila: privately printed.

We Forum. 1982. Various issues.

Chapter 2

Japan's Cultural Diplomacy in the Philippines in the Last Fifty Years: An Assessment

Lydia N. Yu Jose

Almost all scholarly works on Japan's foreign relations with Southeast Asia say that Japan has prioritized economic relations, especially in the first decades after the Second World War. Almost all agree that economic diplomacy is one reason for Japan's postwar economic success; at the same time, however, it caused tension between Japan and Southeast Asia in the 1970s.

This chapter nuances this observation by arguing that while economic diplomacy in the first three decades after the Second World War (1950s to 1970s) failed to win the hearts of Filipinos, Japan's economic development attracted them. Economic development became a source of soft power that made Filipino observers look at Japan with admiration. "Economically developed" became the most frequently mentioned characteristic of Japan, and many were inspired to scrutinize the factors that made it possible. Moreover, many casual observers—and there were more of them than the frequent and close observers, equated the manifestations of economic development, such as the bullet train, elevated highways, cars, and electronic gadgets, with Japanese culture.

Economic development is different from economic diplomacy, which, for Japan in the 1960s through the 1970s meant aggressive trade with and investment in Asia. Economic development embodies and is embodied in Japanese culture. Economic diplomacy, on the other hand, is one of the strategies employed by states to achieve foreign-policy goals. Trade, investment, grants and loans are the usual components of economic diplomacy.

Cultural diplomacy is also a strategy. Its usual components are movies, paintings, literary forms, sculpture, architecture, the state's history, economy, politics, ideology, foods, costumes, science and technology, values, and many more. Cultural diplomacy is the selective dissemination abroad of such components either for the achievement of certain policy goals such as economic development, mutual understanding, or purely for the sake of cultural dissemination.

The second argument of the chapter is that, while Japan focused on economic diplomacy towards the Philippines in the 1950s and 1960s, it used several components of culture, such as sports, arts, education, language, and even the members of the imperial family, to win the hearts of Filipinos, and achieve its economic objectives.

The third point that this chapter stresses is that since the 1980s to the present, at least so far as Philippines-Japan relations are concerned, Japanese culture has reached the Philippines more through unorganized agents such as the Filipino migrants in Japan, than through the Japanese government's cultural diplomacy. A deeper intertwining of economics and culture has developed, in that the Filipino migrant workers become attracted to Japan for economic reasons but in the process become unwitting promoters of Japanese culture.

This chapter focuses on the years between 1956 and 2006. Within these years, the Philippines and Japan concluded three major treaties, namely, the San Francisco Peace Treaty, which restored the relationship between the two countries after the Second World War, the War Reparations Treaty, and the Treaty of Amity, Commerce and Navigation, and the Japan-Philippines Economic Partnership Agreement (JPEPA), which Philippine President Gloria Arroyo and Prime Minister Koizumi Jun'ichiro signed in September 2006 at Helsinki. As of this writing JPEPA is awaiting Senate ratification.

The chapter will use these treaties as points of reference around which cultural diplomacy will be discussed. This approach ensues from the second argument stated above; that is, Japan used cultural diplomacy to achieve economic goals. And since cultural diplomacy as a component of soft power is about attracting followers and supporters, the chapter will identify who in the Philippines became attracted to what.

Japanese Soft Power vis-à-vis the Philippines: Soft Economic Power and Culture

Joseph Nye developed the concept of "soft power" in the late 1980s, when the United States was perceived to be declining in power. He argued that the United States was far from declining, for it was not only the strongest power in the world in terms of military and economic power, but also of soft power (Nye 2004, xi). Soft power is defined as "the ability to get what you want through attraction rather than coercion or payments" (ibid., x). Nye believes that American culture, from the noble values of democracy and human rights to the more mundane consumerism, sex and violence portrayed in Hollywood movies make the United States seductive to many people (ibid., 12).

Nye does not condemn hard power. He is in favor of using it when necessary, but in combination with soft power. What Nye condemns is the use of hard power alone, like President George Bush's unilateral attack on Iraq in the wake of the terrorists' attacks on the United States on 11 September 2000.

Policy, aside from culture, is also a source of soft power. Policy includes economic assistance, scholarships, educational and cultural exchanges, sports, and other diplomatic strategies (ibid., 25–30).

Soft power, Nye says, is available to all states. Even Bin Laden "has soft power for those who believe in the legitimacy of his objectives" (ibid., 2). In other words, as a cliché goes, beauty is in the eye of the beholder.

Nye initially used the concept of soft power in the context of the United States, which has traditionally employed all the three powers:

military, economic, and soft, in various combinations. The most basic formula was to use military might and economic power for the cause of democracy (democracy being an element of attraction). Initially, Nye wanted to argue that in the late 1980s, even though the United States seemed to be weakening in military and economic influence, it still had soft power to get what it wanted. After President Bush's decision to attack Iraq, however, Nye criticized him for depending too much on hard power, thus losing the soft power of the United States.

The concept of soft power in the context of Philippine-Japanese relations operates differently, because in the initial interaction between the Philippines and Japan at the turn of the twentieth century, Japan did not use military power and had only economic power as an element of hard power. Unlike the United States, it had very little soft power to lose in its dealings with the Philippines. Gradually, in the 1930s, it had to build soft power in order to maintain its economic power in the Philippines, and to justify the use of military power in China. Japan used military power against the Philippines only during the Second World War and its occupation of the Philippines (1942–1945). After the Second World War, through Article Nine of its postwar Constitution, Japan adopted the policy of refraining from the use of force to advance its national interests.

Therefore, in the context of Philippine-Japanese relations and, indeed, in the history of Japan's postwar foreign policy in general, hard power for Japan was only economic power (for the United States, it was military and economic). It must be remembered, however, that Nye identifies economic policy as a source of soft power. There is, therefore, a need to stress the difference between economic power as hard power and economic power as soft power. Economic power manifested in the strength of exports, sheer amount of foreign direct investments, size of gross domestic product and gross net profit is hard power. For example, Japanese economic expansion to the Philippines in the 1920s and 1930s became a source of tension between Japan and the United States. Likewise, in the 1960s, Japanese economic penetration of Southeast Asia earned Japan the ire of many

Southeast Asians, and the sobriquet "economic animal" (Sudo 1992, 60). Economic power manifested in the fair amount and beneficial quality of foreign aid for the recipient, fair amount and beneficial quality of foreign direct investment in the host country, and fairness of trade practices is soft power. The Fukuda Doctrine of the late 1970s promised to do these. Simply put, there is a difference between just being rich and how the rich obtain and use wealth.

Additionally for Japan, its ability to modernize and industrialize during the second half of the nineteenth century without losing much of its traditional culture made it attractive to the world. After the Second World War, the economic miracle it achieved in the 1960s became a source of soft power that motivated many developing countries to study Japan. As will be seen below, Japan possesses various potentials for soft power, namely, soft economic power, traditional arts and culture, popular culture, values, its own history of modernizing without entirely Westernizing, and its proverbial ability to quickly rise from the ashes of defeat in the Second World War. In the context of its bilateral relations with the Philippines, the question is whether Japan was able to effectively utilize these potentials.

JAPANESE CULTURAL ASSETS AND LIABILITIES IN THE PHILIPPINES

In spite of centuries of contact with the Philippines, Japan did not have a cultural policy regarding the Philippines. It was only interested in trade, investment, and promotion of Japanese immigration to the Philippines, especially in the 1920s and 1930s (Jose 1998).

A semblance of Japanese cultural diplomacy towards the Philippines began only in the 1930s, and gradually became more active and overt towards the 1940s. It was triggered by a desire to counteract anti-Japanese public opinion about the Japanese invasion of China and public suspicion about Japan's aggressive intentions towards the Philippines, and to protect Japanese trade and Japanese immigration to the Philippines from adverse effects of anti-Japanese public opinion (Jose 1999, 141–44).

The inchoate Japanese cultural diplomacy targeted the Filipino elite, students, and young professionals. Semigovernmental organizations, newspaper companies, and business enterprises invited Filipinos for a minimal fee to visit Japan. Tour participants were guided to regular tourist spots, invited to ikebana exhibitions and tea ceremonies, and given lectures on Japanese history, arts, and culture.

Japanese professors were sent to major Philippine universities to lecture on Japanese economy, history, arts, and culture. Filipino students were invited to Japan to attend student conferences, and Japanese students were sent to the Philippines for the same purpose. The student conferences aimed at mutual cultural understanding.

Japan, however, could only offer what it had. In the 1930s, it had a militaristic, nondemocratic government. Japanese were subjects of the emperor. The male-female relationship was hierarchical, with the woman expected to be submissive to the man. The majority of the Japanese were not Christians. Many Japanese were poor, and just like Filipinos, quite a number dreamt of, and did migrate to, the United States and even to the Philippines.

Tours of Japan did expose a few Filipinos to architecturally beautiful Buddhist temples and Shinto shrines, but at the same time, it stressed the fact that the Japanese were not Christians, and were therefore different from Filipinos. Very few Filipinos at that time appreciated religious plurality. Due to the influence of the Catholic hierarchy, beliefs and practices that went against Christian beliefs were strongly criticized. Thus, while Japanese intellectuals were proud of the samurai ethics or *bushido*, and a few Filipino intellectuals had gained a deeper understanding of it, the Catholic Church in the Philippines strongly disapproved of the Japanese form of suicide called *seppuku*, more commonly known as *hara-kiri*.

Lectures on the emperor system and the relationship between the Emperor and his Japanese subjects could have extolled loyalty, but at the same time, it brought to the surface the undemocratic and nonliberal political system of Japan. By the 1930s, Filipinos had been taught by their American colonizers the values of democracy and political rights.

Still along the concept of democracy and equality, a male Filipino chauvinist could have been attracted to the idea of having a submissive Japanese wife, but such a culture nevertheless clashed with the accepted Filipino norm of respect for womanhood and equality of man and woman before the law, no matter how limited its enforcement at that time. *Madame Butterfly*, an opera by Italian composer Puccini, was translated into Tagalog and serialized in a magazine. This indicates the popularity of the image of a loyal Japanese wife and of committing *seppuku* as proof of loyalty and endless love. Indeed, it was popular among young women of the 1920s and 1930s to don a kimono and have their photo taken in a studio. But *Madame Butterfly* was just a romantic tragedy meant for entertainment, and posing for a photograph garbed in a kimono was just a fad. The kimono or even the more comfortable *yukata* was not worn by Filipino women everyday.

Moreover, Japanese cultural diplomacy reached only a handful of Filipinos. Whatever beauty and attractiveness that this handful of Filipinos admired in bushido, ikebana, Noh, tea ceremony, and other fine Japanese ways of doing things, was simply irrelevant to the majority of Filipinos. To most Filipinos, the cheap and breakable Japanese-made toys, bicycles, fountain pens, and low quality facial make-up and hair dyes embodied Japanese culture.

Towards the 1940s, the Japanese government doubled its efforts at defending the invasion of China and explaining its concept of equal sharing of the resources of the world. But in doing so, Japanese speakers unwittingly revealed their values which were not at all attractive to Filipinos. The more Japan's relationship with the West worsened because of the China question, the more the Japanese criticized the United States and American culture, and the more they did so, the wider the gap between Japanese and Filipino values became. The more they contrasted Japanese industry and the *Yamato damashii*

(Japanese spirit) with the individualistic and materialistic culture of American democracy, the more the militaristic and totalitarian nature of their culture came to the fore. Moreover, Japan's explanations for its invasion of China struck the Philippine mass media as propaganda because of the gap between Japanese actions and Japanese claims.

Consequently, Japan's attempts to introduce Japanese culture had an ambiguous impact. Ikebana was appreciated, but it did not become the Filipino way of arranging flowers. Japanese disgust for individualism and materialism was an indication of undemocratic culture to some Filipinos, but to others, it meant nationalism and efficiency. A member of the first educational tour in 1935 said, "To me one of the most striking social phenomena in the life of the Japanese people is their willingness to sacrifice individual liberty of action and freedom of thought for the sake of national discipline and collective efficiency. . . . Perhaps a combination of both . . . would serve the interests and well being of our commonwealth" (Calica 1935, 106). If others criticized Japanese social values for being different from the Hispanized and Americanized social values of Filipinos, others saw in Japanese values an admirable blend of the modern and the traditional. A journalist wrote: "There seems to be no question that there is today a silent struggle between the ancient and the modern, between the native and the foreign, between tradition and the increasing demand for new things. The ability of Japanese so far to maintain their own culture in the face of advancing modernity reveals the native strength and characteristic individuality of the race" (Farolan 1934, 35). The journalist who wrote this was commissioned by the Japanese Consulate in the Philippines to go to Japan and write about his observations. The same strategy of commissioning Filipino journalists to write about Japan would be employed by the Japanese government in the period immediately following the Second World War.

The Japanese occupation of the Philippines (1942–1945) was the first time the Filipino nation had a first-hand encounter with Japanese culture. Before the war, as mentioned above, Filipinos who had some knowledge of Japan were largely from the elite and those who followed current events in the mass media. But during the Japanese occupation, experience of a culture of discipline, unforgiving punishment even for minor offenses, brutality, ruling through threats, and cowing the people by sowing fear in their hearts, was a national Filipino experience with only a few exceptions.

Filipinos who still remember the war mostly recall Japanese discipline and nationalism. To them, discipline was manifested in the requirement that civilians line up for rides, movies and ration tickets. Filipinos saw in the Kamikaze pilots ultimate nationalism. There were those who admired these characteristics and wished Filipinos were as disciplined and nationalistic as the Japanese. But there were also those who equated discipline with harshness and cruelty, and nationalism with the major cause of Japanese aggression in the Second World War. Filipino reaction to Japanese culture during the war was ambivalent and ambiguous as it was before the Second World War, but the negative impact during and after the war was more predominant. This would be evident in the difficulties the Philippines and Japan encountered in their efforts to normalize their relations after the war.

Ratification of the Peace Treaty and the War Reparations Agreement

The first postwar major negotiations between the Philippines and Japan were over the San Francisco Peace Treaty and the War Reparations Agreement. The Philippine Senate initially did not want to ratify the peace treaty without any agreement on war reparations. Basically, the negotiations revolved around Japan's insistence on paying reparations only according to its ability to pay, and in terms of the Philippine demand to be paid for all the measurable damage and losses that it suffered during the war (Yoshikawa 2003). The Japanese and Philippine governments correctly assessed the stumbling block to the ratification of the two treaties as not mere Japanese and Filipino politicking but as a real reflection of the anti-Japanese mood and public opinion in the Philippines, as well as the sincere desire on the part of Filipinos to be compensated for their wartime losses and sufferings (Meyer 1965, 63). The task for Japan, therefore, was to appease the Filipinos.

In the first half of the 1950s Japan could not use its cultural assets as sources of soft power. Anti-Japanese feeling was too strong to be conquered with displays of ikebana, performance of Noh, origami demonstration, and the like. The Japanese government knew very well they would only be rebuffed. Besides, cultural diplomacy was not affordable to Japan, which was still rebuilding itself from the ashes of war.

Japan was further hampered by fears among its Asian neighbors that it might rearm and become militaristic again. These fears were brought about by the United States' request to Japan to build its army in the wake of the Communist invasion of Korea in 1950.

Japanese cultural diplomacy regarding the Philippines in the 1950s had few resources to draw from. It was hampered by proximity to the Second World War. Moreover, using potential resources presented various dilemmas. If it used the impressive fact that it was fast recovering from the destruction of the Second World War, it would face more demands for bigger reparations. If it used an anticommunist policy, which would be attractive to the Philippines (which was then fighting its local communist adherents and also being threatened by the international domino effect of communist expansion), it might antagonize China and the Soviet Union and jeopardize future relations with them.

Japan used whatever limited resources for cultural diplomacy were available. Sports was one of them. The First Asian Games in New Delhi, India, in March 1951 offered an opportunity for the Philippines and Japan to explore sports as a means of healing the wounds of war (Bitong 1957, 27). Japan garnered the most number of gold, silver, and bronze medals. This was followed by Japanese and Filipino sports matches in Tokyo, Osaka, and Nagoya, the very first of which was in February 1952 in Tokyo (Takamatsu 1952).

Organized by the Japan Basketball Association and sponsored by the Yomiuri Shimbun-sha (Yomiuri Newspaper) with the cooperation of the Japanese Ministry of Foreign Affairs, the Japanese Ministry of Education, and an association of Japanese businessmen, the Firipin Tomo no Kai, the Philippine Air Lines Basketball Team played with several Japanese company and university basketball teams (Japanese-Philippine Basketball Friendship Matches 1952). The aim of the matches was to promote friendship and mutual understanding between the Philippines and Japan (Vargas 1952; Takamatsu 1952). The Second Asian Games were held in Manila in 1953, and the largest group of Japanese was seen in Manila for the first time since the end of the Second World War (Bitong 1957, 27). Again, Japan garnered the most number of gold, silver and bronze medals.

On the part of civil society, there were pen pal clubs ostensibly started by Japanese and Filipino students between 1952 and 1953 (Serrano 1952, 48; Serrano 1953, 48). In January 1953 four Japanese students came to Manila to attend the first postwar Philippine-Japanese student conference (Bitong 1957, 27). Japanese boy scouts participated in the first Philippine National Boy Scouts Jamboree, held in Balara, Quezon City, in 1954 (Jap Boy Scouts 1954, 48).

The Philippine Senate finally ratified the peace treaty and the reparations agreement on 23 July 1956, five years after the Japanese and Philippine governments officially signed the San Francisco Peace Treaty. Sports diplomacy, pen pal clubs, boy scout jamborees, and student conferences did not influence the Senate to ratify the treaties, but they were proofs that Japan did not simply rely on pragmatic economic arguments about why the Philippines should ratify the two treaties. Japan tried cultural strategies in order to resume friendship with the Philippines. On the other hand, the cooperation given by the Philippine presidents and their advisers towards the ratification of the treaties indicates that they were motivated by pragmatic considerations but were hampered by the anti-Japanese public opinion and considerations about the future of their political career. The realities of the Cold War and the promises of trade, aid, grants, loans, and investments in the Reparations Treaty were the factors that made the Senate ratify the San Francisco Peace Treaty and the Reparations Treaty.

Negotiating a Commercial Treaty

The limited results of Japanese cultural diplomacy in the 1950s were evident in the difficulty experienced by Japan in getting the Philippines to conclude a commercial treaty with it.

In the initial years of the implementation of the Reparations Treaty, the Japanese government exerted its utmost efforts to have a commercial treaty with the Philippines signed and ratified. The Japanese government was eager to conclude such a treaty because the Philippines had a stable economy, second only to Japan. On the other hand, Philippine President Carlos P. Garcia wanted the Japanese government to agree to certain adjustments in the implementation of the reparations agreement to enable him to carry out development projects. The Japanese government used Garcia's political need as a bargaining tool to persuade the President to start negotiations for a commercial treaty (Yoshikawa 2003). Garcia gave the signal to begin the negotiations, and shortly after, on 9 December 1960, the two governments signed the Treaty of Amity, Commerce and Navigation. The Japanese Diet ratified it in October 1961. At this point, however, political exchange of favors did not work anymore. The Philippine Senate steadfastly refused to ratify the treaty.

In the 1960s and the 1970s, pending the ratification of the commercial treaty, the Philippine mass media expressed skepticism about the beneficial effects of the treaty on the Philippines. Many commentators revived memories of Japanese expansionism before the Second World War and the Japanese occupation of the Philippines during the war, as a way of warning readers what would happen if the treaty were to be ratified.* It was evident that twenty years or so after the war, negative memories could still be used to arouse suspicion and skepticism about Japanese intentions.

The task for the Japanese government was to present an image of a Japan that was peaceful, modern, friendly, generous, and trustworthy. By the 1960s, this was not an empty image. It was real and possessed a tremendous potential to win the Filipinos' admiration.

In the 1960s Japan was already confident that it could display its economic achievements without fear of being asked to pay huge war reparations. It was determined more than ever to expand markets for its exports and to buy raw materials from its Asian neighbors to feed its manufacturing industry. Hence, if in the 1950s the Philippine economic missions were going to Japan to see if Japan could afford to pay war reparations, in the 1960s Japan was inviting journalists, educators, and artists to see economic development in Japan and write about it back home.

In January 1966 the *Manila Chronicle Magazine*, a weekly, came out with a special on "The New Japan." The cover featured the famous Toshogu Shrine of Nikko. The magazine contained an article by Ileana Maramag, associate editor of the magazine, who had been invited by the Ministry of Foreign Affairs to visit Japan. Escorted by a lady officer of the ministry, she toured Tokyo, Kyoto, and Nara (Maramag 1966, 9). Maramag's article, which begins with "Today Japan Views War with Instinctive Dread and Pursues a Policy of Progress through Peace" (ibid., 6), presented a very positive picture of modern Japan. Another article, "Progress through Education," was written by a professor of commercial law in the University of Santo Tomas who had also been invited by the Japanese government to visit Japan. The article praises Japan's move to review its educational system and see how it could further contribute to economic development, and urges Filipino educators to do the same. The other articles introduce tea ceremony, Japanese music, Noh, a woman novelist, tiny transistors and satellite transmitters, Toyota car, Hotel Okura, and the Japanese shipping industry with quite detailed information and a fair amount of admiration.

One symbol of social change and modernization in Japan which captured the imagination of the world in 1959 was the marriage of Crown Prince Akihito to a commoner, Princess Michiko (former Michiko Shoda), breaking an old tradition which decreed that the crown prince could marry only a person of royal blood. The crown prince broke tradition again when he and Princess Michiko decided against having their son separated from them and reared by nurses and tutors.

In November 1962 the Crown Prince and Princess Michiko visited the Philippines. The announced purpose of the visit was to promote friendship and goodwill. The mass media, however, reported speculations that the more important purpose was to charm public opinion into favoring the ratification of the commercial treaty.

In December 1966 the Japanese Ministry of Foreign Affairs donated to the Ateneo de Manila University the first Japanese Studies Program in the country (Report 1969; Memorandum 1966; see Chapter 4 of this book). The donation included the salaries of the visiting Japanese professors and free tuition for students in the subjects offered by the program. In 1967 the Japan Information and Cultural Center in Manila was established, and became the main source of information about Japan (see Chapter 3 of this book). The center was also given responsibility to screen applicants to the Japanese Government Scholarship, then popularly known as the Mombusho scholarship, and one of the major components of Japan's cultural diplomacy. Shortly after its opening, the Center started offering Japanese language lessons. The Ship for Southeast Asian Youth arrived for the first time in Manila in 1968. It was also in 1968 that the Japanese Garden in Luneta Park was completed.

On the local level, links between sister cities between the Philippines and Japan were forged. It is interesting to note that six of the twenty sister cities identified by Sato (1994, 199–201) were created in the 1960s and 1970s. The purpose of the Japanese local governments (LGU), consistent with Japan's national policy, was to win the goodwill of the Filipinos. Philippine LGUs would not lose anything by positively and cordially responding to the offer of friendship and cultural exchanges. These sister cities were Caba-Oizumi (1964),

Manila-Yokohama (1965), Hanyu-Baguio (1969), Pasig-Marugame (1972), Quezon City-Chiba (1972), and Baguio-Wakkanai (1973).

Except for the fact that all these cultural initiatives happened during the period of waiting for the ratification of the commercial treaty, there is no watertight proof that they were launched with the single purpose of enticing the Philippine government to ratify the commercial treaty. Whether there was a direct connection or not, it was clear that these cultural initiatives did not change the mind of the Philippine Senate. On 2 March 1972, the Senate rejected the resolution for the ratification of the Treaty of Amity, Commerce and Navigation. On 21 September, Marcos declared martial law on the ground of a looming communist threat to the Philippines. He abolished the Senate and the House of Representatives and ruled as a dictator. On 27 December 1973 he unilaterally declared the commercial treaty ratified.

Before martial law, when freedom of speech and of the press was exercised under a democratic government, public opinion was important to foreign policy. There was strong evidence that the public was against the ratification of the commercial treaty and the Senate listened to it. The arguments put forward against the treaty were rebutted by equally plausible arguments. If there was goodwill toward Japan, it would not have been difficult to ratify the treaty. That the treaty had to be declared as ratified by a dictator showed that Japan was attractive not to the Filipino public but to Marcos.

MARTIAL LAW AND THE FUKUDA DOCTRINE

Nine years of martial law (1972–1981) and six more years of dictatorial rule since the lifting of martial law (1981–1986) in the Philippines coincided with the launching of the Fukuda Doctrine in August 1977. The Fukuda Doctrine was meant to dramatically change Japan's economic diplomacy with ASEAN from one of aggressive trade and profitmaking to doubling of economic aid to ASEAN countries, promoting friendship with ASEAN, and cultivating cultural relations (Sudo 1992). The doctrine was Japan's response to anti-

Japanese demonstrations in many ASEAN countries, particularly in Thailand and Indonesia in 1974, as expressions of protest against Japan's unfair trade practices (ibid., 71–72). The impact of the doctrine was less dramatic than its announcement (ibid., 233–34). Economic aid increased, but Japanese trade surplus vis-à-vis all the ASEAN countries generally remained, and the cultural policy was halfheartedly implemented.

The doubling of economic aid benefited Marcos, who implemented a program of extensive infrastructure construction, using foreign loans. In terms of amount, the contribution of Japanese official development assistance (ODA) to Marcos's program which in effect helped to legitimize martial rule averaged only 6 percent of the total external debt of the Philippines between 1973 and 1983. The amount was small, compared to the contributions of the United States (8 percent), the International Monetary Fund (19 percent), and the World Bank (11 percent). On the other hand, it was much easier for Marcos to obtain Japanese ODA and to control its use because of Japan's hesitation to lay down conditions on its loans. US ODA to the Philippines declined in the 1980s, but Japanese ODA increased and Japan replaced the US as the largest aid-giver to the country (Rivera 2003, 525–26).

With the downfall of the Marcos dictatorship, followed by Corazon Aquino's assumption to the presidency in 1986, there was a great deal of optimism about the future course of Philippine democracy and development. Bilateral trade with Japan increased in volume, but the balance of trade continued to be in favor of Japan. Expansion of Japanese ODA to the Philippines was a welcome development for the new administration that had to face the responsibility of carrying out economic and administrative reforms, including the payment of huge foreign debts incurred by Marcos. In July 1989 Japan joined nineteen countries, the Asian Development Bank, and the International Monetary Fund in forging an agreement that came to be known as the Multilateral Aid Initiative (MAI), known in the Philippines as the Philippine Assistance Program (PAP). In the case of Japan, MAI was significant because it agreed to let the World Bank monitor the Philippines' compliance with the conditions of Japanese aid, except for regular Japanese ODA that continued to be managed bilaterally (Rivera 2003, 529).

For ASEAN as an organization, the Fukuda Doctrine, despite its limited impact, was a turning point in its relations with Japan because of the Japanese official vow to give importance to ASEAN and to be more proactive in supporting ASEAN's economic development, political stability vis-à-vis the Indochina problem, and closer cultural relations. However, for a country like the Philippines, it was unfortunate that this important change in Japan's foreign policy happened at the time that the Philippines was not under a democratic government. It was also unfortunate that Japan, under the principle of separating economics from politics, did not discriminate against a dictatorial and corrupt rule. Japanese aid, loans, and investments entered the Philippines, but Marcos had the sole power to decide how to use the loans and the aid, and which crony would win the contracts. As a result, the aspect of Japanese ODA and investments was tainted with corruption. To date, an objective accounting of Japanese economic relations with the Philippines under martial law has yet to be made. Through the MAI, however, the Japanese government was, to a certain extent, able to correct its ODA policy by agreeing to let the World Bank monitor the Philippines' management of ODA.

ELITE AND POPULAR ATTRACTION TO JAPAN

In the 1960s and 1970s Japan accumulated a huge amount of capital through its labor-intensive industrialization. It had performed an economic miracle. In 1968 Japan commemorated the centennial of the Meiji Restoration, inspiring the holding of various conferences on Japanese modernization and the publication of books on the topic by American scholars. Intellectual leaders and students looked up to Japan as a model of nonsocialist, nonviolent modernization. In Asia, the impact on the Philippines must have been most tremendous because of the easy access to American publications on the part of Filipino students and professors.

Japanese modernization was soft power to Philippine government officials and intellectual elites. So were Japanese arts like ikebana, the performing arts, literature, origami, and films. Wives of Philippine Cabinet members usually graced ikebana demonstrations and exhibits (*Japan Bulletin* 1977 [February], 25–26; 1982 [February], 4; 1982 [July], 4). Members of high society, the diplomatic corps, professionals, businessmen, and students were invited to Japanese cultural performances and films at the Cultural Center of the Philippines and the Film Center. Literature and origami were taught to high school teachers (*Japan Bulletin* 1982 [May], 9–10; 1983 [May], 20).

But the majority of Filipinos remained oblivious to developments in Japan and the world. Even university students did not display great enthusiasm for Japan. The Japanese Studies Program in Ateneo attracted only a handful of students. So bad was the student turnout that classes about Japan were not economically viable. As a result, the university, despite the general recognition that Japan was an important model of modernization for the Philippines, hesitated to invest in faculty development and in an undergraduate degree in Japanese Studies. In 1979, the university president wrote: "The basic goals of a strict Japanese Studies Program for majors is out of the question for the Ateneo de Manila. It is not possible to get the students for this, nor are we willing to make the investment of time and money that such a specialized program would require" (Memo 1979). No undergraduate degree in Japanese Studies was established, but the university continued to offer Japanese language along with other foreign languages such as Spanish and French. Elective courses in Japanese history, politics, economics, and foreign relations were also retained. These usually had small classes of a dozen students at the most.

Filipino popular attraction to the rich, industrialized, and modern Japan began only in the 1980s. The factor that propelled it was the high value of the yen. Many Filipinos, attracted by the favorable exchange rate of the yen as against the Philippine peso, went to work in Japan. Migration of Filipino workers to Japan began in the 1970s, but it was in the 1980s that the number of registered Filipinos dramatically increased from over 6,000 in 1981 to close to 50,000 in 1991 (Ministry of Justice Homepage). Moreover, by the mid-1980s, because of the high cost of domestic labor brought about by tremendous economic growth, many Japanese companies relocated to Southeast Asia, in search of cheap labor. Japanese direct investments abroad surged and began to be significant in the Philippines in the late 1980s (Tecson 2003, 464–75). The possibility of employment in Japanese companies after graduating from college became a strong motivation to take up Japanese language and culture as elective subjects.

A number of schools offering Japanese language outside of the university opened at about the same time, catering to all sorts of people, male and female: those who wanted to work in Japan, those who had businesses with Japanese, those who worked or wished to work in Japanese companies, those who were married to Japanese, those who wanted to study in Japan. The economic gap between the Philippines and Japan helped bring about the "Japayuki" phenomenon, an increase in the number of students who want to study in Japan, and an increase in the number of Filipino-Japanese marriages.

One undesirable result of the attraction of Filipino workers to Japan is that some of them continue to stay there even after the expiration of their visas. Another undesirable result is the maltreatment of workers by employers and recruitment agencies. These have caused friction between the two countries, but there is no evidence that these problems have diminished the attraction of Filipino job seekers to Japan.

Thus, while the late 1970s became the turning point of Japan's policy regarding ASEAN as envisioned by the Fukuda Doctrine, the turning point for the Philippines and Japan was the late 1980s. This means that the vision of the Fukuda Doctrine began to show obvious results in the late 1980s. The Filipino middle and upper classes who had some admiration for Japanese culture, particularly for its history of modernization and economic success, were joined by the lower classes who were attracted to economic opportunities in Japan. It was in the 1980s that Japanese popular culture, such as food, karaoke, *manga* and *anime*, began to be appreciated by the lower working class. It may be argued that these aspects of Japanese culture still have not reached the poorest of the poor Filipinos, but compared to the 1950s through the 1970s, Filipinos knowledgeable about Japan and appreciative of things Japanese were less elitist.

The late 1980s was a turning point in Philippines-Japan relations in still another sense. Dissemination of Japanese popular culture by returning Filipino migrant workers in Japan paralleled the cultural diplomacy conducted by the Japan Foundation, whose projects and activities mainly attracted Filipino students, professionals, established intellectuals, and mass media. What college students learned about Japan in the classroom and activities sponsored by the Japan Foundation probably differed from what a neighbor of a Filipina entertainer in Japan learned from the stories of the entertainer returning to the Philippines.

How the gap between elite and popular attraction to Japan impacts on the attractiveness of Japan to the Philippines has not been researched yet. It is clear, however, that the Philippine government appreciates Japan not only as the second biggest source of ODA, investments, and trade, but also as a destination of thousands of Filipino workers every year, who regularly send much-needed remittances to their families back home.

As a result, the Philippine government has become an important supporter of Japan in international affairs. The impact of Japan's soft economic power on the Philippine government was seen in the support given by the Philippines to many of the Japanese goals in the United Nations and regional organizations. In 1995 the Philippines withdrew its bid for a nonpermanent seat in the Security Council in favor of Japan (Villacorta 2003, 587). The Philippines supports Japan's current bid for a permanent seat in the Security Council (ibid., 588). In the ASEAN, the Philippines supports Japan's participation as a dialogue partner.

The Japan-Philippines Economic Partnership Agreement

After the ratification of the commercial treaty, the Philippines and Japan did not sign any treaty of significance until the signing of the Japan-Philippines Economic Partnership Agreement (JPEPA) on 9 September 2006 in Helsinki. Unlike the San Francisco Peace Treaty, the Reparations Treaty, and the Treaty of Amity, Commerce and Navigation, which were rigorously debated and opposed by public opinion, the JPEPA did not see much public discussion. In a rare mention of it in newspapers, objections focused on unequal benefits that the Philippines and Japan would get from the agreement. But the criticisms were expressed without any reference to the Second World War or a hint of anti-Japanese sentiment. On the contrary, the critical remarks seemed to target the Philippine government more than they targeted the Japanese government. The political opposition and the Fair Trade Alliance, a multisectoral NGO, criticized and still criticizes the Philippine government for lack of transparency on the details of the agreement (*PDI* 16 June 2005, B-6; 17 June 2005, B-1). Several weeks after the news of its signing in Helsinki, several dailies carried news that through the agreement, the Japanese government would export without tariff hazardous materials to the Philippines (*PDI* 26 October 2006, A-1, A-13; *Philippine Star* 26 October 2006, 1; 11). The Philippine Senate, in response, urged the Philippine president to submit the agreement to the Senate for scrutiny.

While bilateral free trade is provided for in the agreement, it is of secondary importance, at least from the point of view of the Philippine government, to an understanding that enabling laws of the agreement would allow the entry of Filipino information technology (IT) workers, nurses, and caregivers to Japan. Before these new types of workers can enter Japan, they will have to learn the Japanese language and show proof of proficiency by passing the Japanese government's Japanese language-proficiency test. Such a requirement is certainly necessary to assure efficient performance, but there is more to it. The requirement would open an opportunity for the Japanese government to push for the learning of Japanese and thus further promote its wider use in Asia, if not the whole world.

The signing of the JPEPA signifies the deepening of the intertwining relationship between economics and culture which began in the late 1980s. JPEPA embodies the close relationship between economics and culture more than the earlier treaties between the Philippines and Japan. Fifty years after the resumption of Philippines-Japan relations, the two states signed a treaty that attests to the fact that the economic needs of Filipinos create opportunities for Japan to promote Japanese culture, especially the Japanese language. From the 1950s through the 1970s Japan tried to use cultural diplomacy to achieve economic goals; from the 1980s through the present, Japan's economic stature and capability have been the factors that reinforce the spread of Japanese culture. The agents are not just Japanese but Filipinos as well.

Conclusion

The cultural diplomacy that Japan used in the 1950s through the 1970s did not significantly change the unsympathetic Philippine public opinion about Japan. Negative memories of the Second World War lingered and the mass media often referred to them as a means of illustrating their objections to the San Francisco Peace Treaty, the War Reparations Treaty, and the Treaty of Amity, Commerce and Navigation. The treaties were finally ratified, not as a result of Japanese cultural diplomacy but because of pragmatic considerations, such as the prospects for grants, loans, trade, and investment.

This shows that soft power in the form of cultural diplomacy is not as potent as soft economic power as far as Japan's ability to make the Philippines do what it wishes is concerned.

On the other hand, the cultural diplomacy that Japan launched from the 1950s through the 1970s has not been wasted. It exposed the Filipino upper and middle classes to highbrow Japanese culture.

Such an exposure was not the factor that made the Philippine Senate ratify the treaties, but it was nonetheless a cultural capital that contributed to the Filipino elite's understanding of Japan.

The Japanese experience of modernizing without losing the traditional culture in the last half of the nineteenth century and the Japanese economic miracle of the 1960s are aspects of the Japanese culture admired by Filipino intellectuals. This should be distinguished from the aggressive economic diplomacy Japan embarked on from the 1950s through the 1970s, which earned the ire of Southeast Asians, including Filipinos. There were no violent protests in Manila, as there were in Bangkok and Jakarta, but this was mainly because the Philippines was under martial law.

Filipino appreciation of Japan assumed a wider social base only in the 1980s, when thousands of Filipinos sought employment in Japan. To them, the attraction of Japan was basically economic opportunity. These Filipino workers go back to the Philippines and unwittingly become agents of the spread of Japanese culture in the Philippines. The popular culture that they appreciate and bring to the Philippines is different from the high culture that the Japan Foundation promotes. Such a difference has not yet overtly figured in the Philippines' foreign policy concerning Japan, but the Philippine government recognizes that Japan is an important destination of Filipino migrant workers, and a source of much-needed remittances. This, again, is soft economic power.

The turning point of Philippines-Japan relations was the late 1980s in terms of the widening of the social base of Filipinos who had some knowledge of Japan, and in terms of the tighter intertwining of economics and culture. In the late 1980s there was a great demand for Japanese-language teachers and for information about Japan. The cultural diplomacy that Japan launched in the decades before the 1980s, and the institutions created, enabled both Japan and the Philippines to meet these demands.

In September 2006 the Philippines and Japan signed the JPEPA, an agreement that is significant for embodying the intertwining of economics and culture. Filipino IT workers and caregivers will be allowed to enter Japan, but one of the conditions is a high level of Japanese-language proficiency. The Philippines' need for job opportunities is now officially an opportunity for the Japanese government to promote the Japanese language abroad.

The case of Japan's cultural diplomacy in the Philippines in the last fifty years shows that cultural diplomacy does not always produce the desired results; neither does it produce immediate results. It is nevertheless a valuable capital that is useful for its own sake and that may become useful for other purposes in due time.

Note

* The critical tone of the commentaries was obvious in their titles: "Must We Have Roads and Peace at the Price of our Self-Respect?" (*Weekly Graphic* 1967, 1–2); "Japanese Economic Penetration" (Alegre 1967, 17, 22); "A Second Japanese Invasion" (Almario 1968, 10–12, 72); "Remember the 'Hayun Maru'" (Barranco 1970, 3, 22).

References

Alegre, Aurelio D. 1967. "Japanese Economic Penetration." *Examiner*. 26 November.

Almario, Manuel F. 1968. "A Second Japanese Invasion." *Graphic*. 22 May.

Barranco, Vic. 1970. " Remember the 'Hayun Maru.'" *Examiner*. 25 April.

Bitong, Ernesto T. 1957. "The Japanese are Back!" *Philippines Free Press*. 18 May.

Calica, Pio. 1935. *Japan Footnotes*. [Manila]: publisher unknown.

Farolan, Modesto. 1934. *Japan at a Glance: Travel Impressions, a Study in Japan-Philippine Relations*. Manila: publisher unknown.

"Jap Boy Scouts in National Jamboree." 1954. *Philippines Free Press*. April.

Japan Bulletin. Various dates.

Japanese-Philippine Basketball Friendship Matches brochure. 1952. 2–12 February. (Author's personal copy).

Jose, Lydia N. Yu. 1998. "Philippines-Japan Relations: The Revolutionary Years and a Century Hence." In *Philippine External Relations: A Centennial Vista*, ed. Aileen Baviera, and Lydia N. Yu Jose. Manila: Foreign Service Institute, Department of Foreign Affairs.

________. 1999. *Japan Views the Philippines*. Quezon City: Ateneo de Manila University Press.

Maramag, Ileana. 1966. "Progress through Peace." *Chronicle Magazine*. 29 January, 6–11.

Memo. 1979. Bienvenido F. Nebres, Dean, School of Arts and Sciences, Ateneo de Manila University, to Joseph Pittau and Michael Yanase, 28 August.

Memorandum. [1966]. The Japanese Studies Program, Ateneo de Manila University.

Meyer, Milton Walter. 1965. *A Diplomatic History of the Philippine Republic*. Honolulu: University of Hawaii Press.

Ministry of Justice Homepage (Japan). http://www.moj.go.jp/PRESS/010613-1/010613-1-3.html. Viewed on 1 October 2001.

"Must We Have Roads and Peace at the Price of Our Self-Respect?" 1967. *Weekly Graphic*, 1 November.

Nakagawa Toru. 1953. "Japan-Philippine Relations." *Fookien Times Yearbook*.

Nye, Joseph, Jr. 2004. *Soft Power*. New York: Public Affairs.

PDI (*Philippine Daily Inquirer*). 2005. June; 2006. October.

Philippine Star. 2006. October.

Report. 1969. The Director [Haruo Tsuru] of the Japanese Studies Program of the Ateneo de Manila University. February.

Rivera, Temario C. 2003. "The Politics of Japanese ODA in the Philippines, 1971–1999." In *Philippines-Japan Relations,* ed. Ikehata Setsuho and Lydia N. Yu Jose. Quezon City: Ateneo de Manila University Press.

Sanvictores, Philip. 1993. "A School is Born." *The Philippines-Japan Digest*. Vol. XVIII, No. 1 (February).

Sato Torao. 1994. *Firipin to Nihon: Koryu 500 nen* [Five Centuries of Filipino-Japanese Relations]. Tokyo: The Simul Press.

Serrano, Paquito. 1952. "Japan Uses Her Youth." *Philippines Free Press*. August.

________. 1953. "Japan and Her Pen Pal Clubs." *Philippines Free Press*. January.

Sudo Sueo. 1992. *The Fukuda Doctrine and ASEAN*. Singapore: Institute of Southeast Asian Studies.

Takamatsu (Prince). 1952. Message in Japanese-Philippine Basketball Friendship Matches brochure, 2–12 February. (Author's personal copy).

Tecson, Gwendolyn R. 2003. "Postwar Japanese Direct Investments." In *Philippines-Japan Relations,* ed. Ikehata Setsuho and Lydia N. Yu Jose. Quezon City: Ateneo de Manila University Press.

Vargas, [Jorge B.]. 1952. Message in Japanese-Philippine Basketball Friendship Matches brochure, 2–12 February. (personal copy of the author)

Villacorta, Wilfrido V. 2003. "Political Relations between Japan and the Philippines during the Aquino and Ramos Administrations." In *Philippines-Japan*

Relations, ed. Ikehata Setsuho and Lydia N. Yu Jose. Quezon City: Ateneo de Manila University Press.

Weekly Graphic. 1967.

Yoshikawa Yoko. 2003. "War Reparations Implementation, Reparations-Secured Loans and a Treaty of Commerce." In *Philippines-Japan Relations,* ed. Ikehata Setsuho and Lydia N. Yu Jose. Quezon City: Ateneo de Manila University Press.

Chapter 3

The Japan Information and Cultural Center in the Philippines

Cecilia P. Tolentino

The Press and Cultural Office of the Embassy of Japan in the Philippines became the Japan Information Center (JIC) in April 1967, on the same day that it obtained its own office on the ground floor of the new, white, four-story Filinvest Building located near the San Andres Rotunda, at the corner of Quirino Avenue and Taft Avenue. The JIC was formally inaugurated in September 1967. It was a two-day affair, the first being attended by prominent Filipino government officials and members of the diplomatic corps, the second by other guests. The first director of JIC was the *muy simpatico* Spanish-speaking Sakamoto Jutaro.

In those days, bad feelings and mistrust of Japan were widespread and intense among many Filipinos, in contrast to the friendly attitude toward Japan today, with few displays of antipathy. It was, therefore, in order to lighten these feelings and promote mutual understanding that the JIC undertook several activities immediately after its inauguration, basically providing information about Japan and promoting Japanese culture.

Information Center

JIC provides the working force for the Embassy of Japan both for cultural and press matters. It coordinates with the Philippine Government and private entities whenever the Japanese Government sends goodwill missions or groups of cultural performers to the Philippines. JIC is the office approached by Filipino media for information about Japan, as well as for necessary procedural matters whenever they have to go to Japan. JIC manages the programs of the Japanese Ministry of Foreign Affairs for the Philippine press, and is usually the office that sends official invitations to journalists and TV stations.

On the other side of the coin, JIC facilitates the process of obtaining accreditation from the Philippine Government for Japanese mass-media personnel who want to cover events about the Philippines. JIC becomes especially preoccupied with such matters during visits by Japanese prime ministers, Cabinet members, and other dignitaries, who are usually accompanied by a large number of Japanese journalists, or during big news events like the first EDSA People Power revolution.

Establishment of a Japanese Language School

JIC opened a Japanese-language school, hoping discreetly to achieve a goal, the establishment of a school for Japanese children. Under the old Constitution of the Philippines (1935), establishment of schools exclusively for foreigners, other than the American School, was not allowed. The Japanese government wanted to open a school for the growing number of Japanese children in Metro Manila but could not because of this constitutional prohibition. Thus, in the Note Verbale to the Department of Foreign Affairs about the opening of Japanese-language classes for Filipino students and professionals, it was mentioned that classes for Japanese children would also be held in the same school. The second and third floors of the Filinvest Building were utilized for this purpose until the old constitution was amended.*

Meanwhile, JIC acquired another "c" and became JICC when its name was changed to Japan Information and Cultural Center, shortly before it moved to a new location along Buendia Avenue (now Gil Puyat) in Bel-Air, Makati. It shared the quarters with the Japanese Embassy. When the Japanese Embassy moved to its present location on Roxas Boulevard, JICC moved with it, but a great decision had to be made about the Japanese Language School attached to JICC. Among the options available, it was decided to separate the school from JICC, and to transfer the ownership and operation of the school to the Philippines-Japan Friendship Foundation. Then under the leadership of Jose S. Laurel, son of Jose P. Laurel (president of the Japanese sponsored Philippine Republic) and former ambassador to Japan, the Philippines-Japan Friendship Foundation opened the Nihongo Center Foundation. The Nihongo Center holds classes in the university belt of Manila and in Makati.

JAPAN BULLETIN

The publication of the monthly *Japan Bulletin* was a big plus in the promotion of mutual understanding between the Philippines and Japan. Copies were distributed to almost all schools and libraries throughout the Philippines. Although the printing was not as advanced as it is today, its cover, which was printed in Japan and sent to Manila, was colorful. The publication contained interesting articles on Japan and was eagerly read by thousands of recipients, especially in the provinces. JIC, as it was still called, tried to make it as interesting as possible, at one time featuring monthly Nihongo lessons written by the principal of the Japanese Language School and myself. Articles in Tagalog also appeared in some issues.

Japan Bulletin has continued to be a vehicle of interesting news about Japan and Philippines-Japan relations, although it no longer comes out regularly. With the coming of the computer age, the Embassy of Japan now disseminates news and information through its website, which was started and is managed by JICC.

GOODWILL MISSIONS

In the late 1960s rich Japanese prefectures like Hyogo and Kanagawa would send goodwill missions to the Philippines. Ships would bring in hundreds of Japanese students. To manage these visits, JIC would coordinate with the Department of Foreign Affairs, the city governments of Manila and Pasay, the Department of Tourism, and other government authorities. They would usually form committees to plan a schedule of activities for the youths, including home visits to Filipino families. These activities became the foundation of the present Ship for Southeast Asian Youth Program, which includes not only Japanese but also youths from Southeast Asian countries.

The Japanese Government's Scholarship Program

The Japanese Government began giving scholarships to Filipinos in 1954. Selection of the Filipino recipients of the scholarship, then popularly referred to as the Mombusho (Ministry of Education) Scholarship, was jointly handled by the Philippines' Department of Foreign Affairs, Civil Service Commission, and the National Economic Development Authority (NEDA). Upon the creation of JIC, selection of scholars was transferred to it. Sakamoto, the first director of JIC, signed a memorandum of agreement to this effect with the three Philippine government agencies that previously did the selection.

In September 1967 the Embassy of Japan put out full-page advertisements in major Philippine newspapers about the available scholarships and the new selection procedure. The paid advertisements included my article about my experiences as a student in Japan from 1964 to 1966. Thus started JICC's annual screening of applicants for the scholarship. Representatives from the Japanese Ministry of Education in Tokyo and prominent Filipino professionals in different academic fields comprised the screening committees. Miss Lydia N. Yu, now Dr. Lydia N. Yu Jose, the current director of the Japanese Studies Program of Ateneo de Manila University, was one of the recipients of the scholarship under the new procedure. She was awarded the scholarship in 1969. In later years the original undergraduate and research grants were expanded by additional grants for technical college, undergraduate professional training schools *(senmon gakko)*, in-service training for teachers, the Asian Youth Fellowship (AYF) and the Young Leaders Program (YLP) for graduate students and professionals.

Around ten years after the start of the scholarship program, Filipino alumni of Japanese universities who studied under the scholarship program formed an association with the encouragement and financial support by the Embassy of Japan. Thus, in 1973 was formed the Philippine Association of Japanese Ministry of Education Scholars (PHILAJAMES).

At that time the Japanese Government recognized the importance of mobilizing the intellectual elites of Southeast Asia, especially the alumni of Japanese universities, and exerted efforts to achieve this. In 1974 the Ministry of Foreign Affairs inaugurated the first reunion (*tsudoi*) of Southeast Asian alumni of Japanese universities and colleges by inviting some of them, together with their husbands and wives, to a two-week tour of Japan. The tsudoi is now an annual undertaking of the Ministry of Foreign Affairs, but it has become smaller in scale, for spouses are no longer invited.

The annual tsudoi became the springboard for the creation of the Philippine Federation of Japan Alumni (PHILFEJA) in July 1976. PHILFEJA is the umbrella organization of all associations of Filipino alumni of Japanese universities, regardless of whether the members were recipients of Japanese government scholarships or not. Finally, alumni of Japanese universities from all over Southeast Asia formed the ASEAN Council of Japan Alumni (ASCOJA).

With the expansion of ASEAN from the original six members to the present ten, the annual reunion of alumni of Japanese universities from Southeast Asia also expanded in the number of participating countries. Likewise, the membership of ASCOJA also expanded to include all the ASEAN members.

MOVIES AND DOCUMENTARY FILMS

From 1967 to the early 1970s, one of the effective ways to introduce Japan to the Filipinos was through Japanese documentary films and drama movies. JIC had a movie van with a generator which toured practically all the provinces in the Philippines from Northern Luzon to Mindanao, traveled from town to town, showing movies at the town plaza in the evenings. In places where there was no electricity and therefore no movie houses, these movie presentations were always welcomed by thousands of children and adults.

Documentaries on Japanese culture were fully utilized by Philippine TV stations. Schools all over the country borrowed from JIC sixteen-millimeter films to be shown to their students.

Records of the Japanese Ministry of Foreign Affairs during those years would attest to the fact that the Japanese Embassy in the Philippines, through JIC, was one of the most active in this kind of public relations activity among the Japanese embassies and consulates all over the world.

Ikebana, the Art of Flower Arrangement

In the early years of JIC, the Japanese Government sent several ikebana missions to the Philippines from the various ikebana schools: Ohara, Sogetsu, Ikenobo, and others. Although I had no chance to study this art of flower arrangement while a student in Japan, I learned its rudiments by acting as interpreter for the ikebana masters (*sensei*) who were sent to the Philippines. Ikebana demonstrations were held not only in the JIC audiovisual room but also in different universities in Cebu City, Cagayan de Oro City, and Davao City, with the assistance of the local chapters of Ikebana International in those cities. Unlike at present, when materials for demonstrations are commercially available, in those days they had to be obtained from private gardens. The officers of the local chapters of Ikebana International allowed us to cut plenty of flowers, twigs, leaves, and branches from their beautiful gardens.

Other Cultural Activities

In addition to the above, which have been the more-or-less regular continuing activities of JICC, except for the Japanese Language School which has been transferred to the Philippines-Japan Friendship Foundation, JICC was instrumental in the promotion of special cultural events. Among the most unforgettable cultural presentations I encountered was the Japanese opera "Yuzuru," Japan's contribution to the inaugural opening of the Cultural Center of the Philippines in 1968. And again, in June 1990, the Japanese Government brought the Grand Kabuki to the Filipino audience. In 1986 JICC helped in the launching of the first annual Philippines-Japan Friendship Month. The annual event has undergone several changes in name, from the original one, to Philippines-Japan Cultural Festival, to the present Philippines-Japan Festival.

Since the Japan Foundation established an office in Manila in 1997, much of the cultural activities that used to be initiated, managed, and completed by JICC have been undertaken by the Japan Foundation Manila Office. JICC often coordinates and cooperates with it.

Conclusion

Through various activities, JICC has continued promoting goodwill and friendship between the Philippines and Japan. Even in the years since the ratification of the Treaty of Amity, Commerce, and Navigation between the two countries in 1973, which highlighted the economic aspect of the bilateral relations, JICC has remained an important arm of the Embassy of Japan in the Philippines for bridging the cultures of the two countries.

Although I am no longer with JICC, I know that in the thirty-eight years that I was part of its daily activities, JICC did its share for the betterment of diplomatic relations between the Philippines and Japan.

Note

* On 16 April 2000 the Manila Japanese School opened classes in its present location in Fort Bonifacio Global City, after moving out of Filinvest Building in the late 1970s to be relocated in Levitown Subdivision in Parañaque City.

Chapter 4

The First Japanese Studies Program in the Philippines: Archival Research plus Personal Vignettes

Lydia N. Yu Jose

Japan and the Philippines resumed trade soon after the Second World War. This was partly due to the United States' insistence, for it feared that if the Japanese economy was not rebuilt, Japan might fall prey to communism. Resumption of trade with neighboring countries was one of the pillars of the Japanese economy, and the Philippines, now having "special relations" with the United States, and also fighting communism, was the most logical country to be advised by the United States to resume trade with Japan. Moreover, the reality of the situation in the Philippines was that if the Philippines continued to refuse to trade with Japan, it might, in the end, lose the opportunity to other Southeast Asian countries. Thus, limited trade started in 1947 and it gradually expanded (*RP Official Gazette* 1948, 5). Japanese investments followed towards the end of 1950, but were still limited and quite controversial (see Chapter 2 of this book).

In the 1960s, after Japan achieved the economic miracle, the Japanese Government launched low-key cultural diplomacy, side by side with the more obvious economic thrust. In 1966 the Japanese government donated Japanese Studies Programs to several countries in Asia, namely, the Philippines, Hong Kong, Thailand, Malaysia, Indonesia, and India (Report of the Director [Haruo Tsuru] 1969; Memorandum from the JSP 1966).

It is interesting to note, however, that the Japanese Government resumed cultural relations with the Philippines as early as the mid-1960s, despite the fact that the Second World War in the Philippines was the most violent and bloody in the whole of Southeast Asia and that Filipinos offered the most stubborn resistance to the Japanese invading army. One would think that Japan would have waited a little bit longer before launching a cultural program in the Philippines. But the Japanese Government offered to open in Ateneo de Manila, a Jesuit university, a Japanese Studies Program in 1966, just about twenty years after the end of the war. The objectives of this donation were to promote understanding between Japan and the Philippines, and to encourage the academic study of Japanese affairs and culture (Report of the Director [Haruo Tsuru] 1969; Memorandum from the JSP, 1966).

This chapter will narrate the development of the first Japanese Studies Program in the Philippines. Japanese Studies Program in this essay refers to the institution in a university that offers various subjects on Japan and is established with the support of the Japanese government. The narration aims to bring out the dynamics of interactions between two cultures in an academic setting; between an academic institution with a clear vision and mission, and the Japanese government, equally imbued with its own goals. As the narrative develops, it will also reveal the intertwining of economics and cultural diplomacy. Much of the narration is based on archival research, but a portion of it is based on the author's personal interaction with some of the visiting Japanese professors.

THE FIRST STEPS

The Japanese government offered to Ateneo de Manila University (hereafter, Ateneo) a program wherein the Japanese Government would send visiting Japanese professors to the Philippines.[1] The Japanese government would pay the salaries of these professors for four years, after which, the program should have been able to support local faculty and the head of the program, now called director (Memorandum from the JSP 1966). On 5 July 1966 the Japanese cultural attaché visited the vice-president for academic affairs of the Ateneo to finalize plans for the visiting professors from Japan. The cultural attaché was assured by the vice-president that office space and facilities, office supplies, and secretarial assistants could be provided by the Ateneo, and that a visiting professor would teach at least six units (six hours a week) a semester. The vice-president for academic affairs also thought that it might be possible for the visiting professors to have living accommodations on campus (Memo of John F. Doherty 1966). It turned out that this was not possible; the Ateneo gave them a housing allowance, instead.

The visiting professors arrived on 14 December 1966, and were ready to start teaching the following day (Memo to all units and department heads 1966). The subjects they would teach were "The Development of Japanese Economy," "Post-war Development of Japanese Economy," and "Japanese Language in Culture." They were all tuition-free, but students who would successfully complete a subject could get a three-unit credit. The university officials issued memos encouraging the academic departments to recommend these subjects to their students (Announcement from the Dean 1966). The memos pointed out the advantages of learning the culture and language of Japan: Business relations between the Philippines and Japan would continue to expand, and there were many opportunities for scholarship and research fellowships in Japanese universities for those who had mastered the Japanese language.

The formal ceremony for the inauguration of the program was held on 24 February 1967. Cocktails and a showing of a documentary film on the visit of Philippine president Ferdinand Marcos to Japan followed the congratulatory speeches and expressions of gratitude by Japanese government representatives and university officials.

Why establish a Japanese Studies Program in 1966? It may be theorized that the Japanese government's decision was due to a combination of two factors. First, it had hoped that through a cultural policy such as this, the Treaty of Amity, Commerce and Navigation would be ratified (see Chapter 2 of this book). If ratified, it would validate the legality of the few Japanese investments in the Philippines and further give them a boost. It would also promote Japanese trade. Second, the Japanese government might have thought that since Marcos was friendly to Japan, the time was ripe to launch a cultural policy in the Philippines. One of the components of Marcos' foreign policy was to diversify Philippine foreign relations instead of just maintaining a close alliance with the United States. He paid Japan a state visit on 28–30 September 1966.

The Uphill Climb

Five years passed, and the Ateneo was supposed to have developed local faculty members of the Japanese Studies Program, but there was still no Filipino faculty member who could teach the Japanese language.[2] The director of the Japanese Studies Program was still a Japanese professor sent from Japan. The program was not yet financially viable. The subjects it offered attracted very few students, despite the fact that they were tuition-free.[3] On top of this, in 1973 the university stopped the housing subsidy it was giving to the visiting professors (Report of the Director 1971).

Up to 1974, all the visiting professors of the program came from the International Christian University (ICU). This might have been because the first group of professors came from ICU, and since the choice of who should be sent next was basically dependent on the recommendations of those who had been to the Ateneo, the momentum of recruiting the visiting professors from ICU continued, until there was no more faculty member from that university who could come.[4]

Thus, in June 1974, it was evident that the Japan Foundation (created in 1972, and to which the Ministry of Foreign Affairs transferred this aspect of its cultural diplomacy) was no longer willing to continue sending a visiting Japanese teacher of the Japanese language. Citing as a reason the lack of a suitable replacement for the visiting

Japanese professor who was scheduled to return to Japan, the Japan Foundation requested Ateneo to appoint a local faculty member (Letter of Bienvenido F. Nebres 1974). The Ateneo was able to hire a Japanese-Filipina (her father was a Filipino) instructor. The Japan Foundation agreed to pay her basic salary (despite the fact that in the first agreement, salary support was to end after the first four years of the program) on condition that she would be a permanent faculty member of the Ateneo, and that in the future, the university would shoulder all her salaries and benefits (Letter from Tadashi Inumaru 1974). Finally, after more than seven years, the Japanese Studies Program had one permanent faculty member.

By this time, however, the three Filipino faculty members who had been shared by other academic departments of the university with the program had left the program for various reasons, among which were personal incompatibility with the Japanese faculty and irreconcilable views regarding duties and responsibilities of the Japanese faculty.[5] The one who was recruited in the third or fourth year of the program gave up his interest in Japanese history, for he was burdened with preparation for other history courses—he finally left academe; the second one who joined in 1970 distanced herself from the program after only a couple of years, and the third, who joined in 1971, left the program after three or four years.

The director of the program was still Japanese, sent from Japan on a Japan Foundation salary, but the time came when Ateneo had to appoint a Filipino: it appointed a Filipino Jesuit priest in Sophia University in Tokyo to act as director-in-absentia. Appointment of someone in Tokyo was considered convenient because he was right where the headquarters of the Japan Foundation was and could therefore easily consult with the Foundation officials about the future of the Japanese Studies Program (Memo of Bienvenido F. Nebres 1979). For direct supervision in the Philippines, the program was put directly under the Dean of the College of Arts and Sciences.

From around the 1980s, the Japan Foundation dispatched visiting Japanese professors who stayed for a semester or two. They were no longer from ICU but from other Japanese universities, mostly from Sophia University. They taught mostly social science subjects such as Political Science, History, Sociology, and others.

The first Japanese Studies Program in the Philippines experienced difficulties in its infancy and early adulthood. At first glance, it would seem that the difficulty was due to the incompatible goals of the Ateneo and of the Japanese government (by this time, alternately identified with the Japan Foundation). The Japan Foundation had thought of a program or department of Japanese Studies that would produce graduates who majored in Japanese Studies. On the other hand, an undergraduate or graduate degree in Japanese Studies was far from the mind of the President of Ateneo, who understood the program to consist mainly of teaching the Japanese language, teaching of mostly social science subjects by visiting Japanese professors, and joint research. A degree in Japanese Studies was out of the question because there were no students for it, and the Ateneo was not willing to invest time and money on such a program (Memo of Bienvenido F. Nebres 1979).

That was the problem at first glance, but looking at it deeply, one can ask, why were there no students? This was the real problem, because if there were students, Ateneo, any other university for that matter, would be willing to invest time and money in a course of study on Japan.

There were no students because there were no job opportunities for graduates majoring in Japanese Studies, or even those with only skills in the Japanese language. This was true even up to the late 1970s.

There were also minor problems. One, reflective of the growing gap between the Japanese and the Philippine economy, was that the Japanese-Filipina who was initially paid by the Japan Foundation, and was eventually put on the payroll of the Ateneo, had to make do with a much lower salary (already high by Philippine standards). Another one, reflective of the impact of Japan's cultural nationalism between the 1930s and 1940s, was that almost all the Japanese visiting professors were not fluent in English, the medium of instruction in Philippine universities. This was a particularly acute problem in the Ateneo, known then for "Arneo English," a compliment referring to the almost impeccable English vocabulary and diction of its faculty and students. To address the language problem, the Japan Foundation offered to send American experts on Japan. The Ateneo, however, was not amenable to this, for the intercultural exchange, which was the key factor in the program, "had to be made between natives of the two different cultures" (Letter of Bienvenido F. Nebres 1973). And still another one, already mentioned above, was Ateneo's inaction on the request of the Japan Foundation to appoint a Filipino director. But from the Ateneo president's point of view, this issue was not the real issue. The deeper issue, as mentioned above, was the difference between the goals and priorities of the Ateneo and of the Japan Foundation (Memo of Bienvenido F. Nebres 1979).

Furthermore, it should be repeated here, the much deeper and more real problem than the difference between the Ateneo's and the Japan Foundation's views of Japanese Studies in the Philippines, and the other minor problems mentioned above, was the lack of job opportunities for graduates who were experts in the subject of things Japanese. They therefore lacked the motivation to engage in Japanese studies.

Personal interaction

All the ten directors of the Japanese Studies Program in Ateneo from December 1966 to April 1978 came from ICU. One of them, Tsuru Haruo, professor of Psychology, served for two terms (July 1967 to February 1969 and June 1971 to December 1971). The director who perhaps had the least problems was the first director, Hisatake Masao (December 1966 to June 1967) because the program was newly established and problems were not evident yet. He was succeeded by Professor Tsuru, at the time when the program was supposed to fly on its own, but was not showing any sign of it. He came back in June 1971 as the fifth director, when the program was supposed to have flown on its own, but was still on the ground. On his shoulders fell the heavy responsibility of developing the program.

As a young faculty member then of the Department of Political Science, I saw how Professor Tsuru agonized over the problems of the program. He was a man of few words, but at times of deep frustration, he would share with me the problems being faced by the Japanese Studies Program. He told me that the program should have been opened in the University of the Philippines (UP), not the Ateneo. At that time I took this as a mere expression of extreme exasperation. Only in March of 2007 did I find out that the program was actually offered to UP first, but UP turned it down because the members of the committee then in charge of talking with the Japanese delegation did not like the idea of having visiting Japanese professors teach subjects about Japan (Prof. Benito Lim, casual conversation 2007). Such a stand should be taken in the context of the time: the Second World War had happened only about twenty years before.

The other Japanese directors I had opportunities to interact with were Hoshino Akira (December 1971–June 1972), a psychologist like Professor Tsuru, Kasai Minoru (June 1972–October 1973), known as "the saint" for his stoic demeanor, and Hara Kimi (April 1975–May 1976), the only lady Japanese director the Japanese Studies Program ever had. At this point, it should be mentioned that almost all the visiting Japanese professors, including directors in Ateneo, experienced culture shock at seeing that the faculty was predominantly female.

I still remember the New Year's eve Professor and Mrs. Hoshino spent in our home. They were so amazed at the colorful fireworks and noisy firecrackers. In Japan, New Year's eve is very quiet, almost like Holy Week in the Philippines. Professor Hara, on the other hand, surprised me with an exquisite cloisonné days after she got out of the hospital. She had met a minor car accident, and I visited her in the hospital. I learned later that it is a Japanese practice to give a token of appreciation to someone who visits you in the hospital.

Yoshikawa Yoko was the first visiting instructor of Japanese language. She drove a second-hand car on campus, sometimes with Professor Tsuru and Mr. Aonuma Kiyoshi, professor of Japanese

Politics and Economy. But the two male professors would sit in the back, and only Yoko would be in front, driving like a hired chauffeur. The Ateneo community found this funny, but it was explained to them that in Japan, it is perfectly fine for the car owner who drives his/her own car to have all his/her companions sit in the back. He/she would not be mistaken for a hired driver for few families in Japan have hired drivers anyway.

Yoko was a fresh college graduate of ICU when she came to the Ateneo. I was then a graduate student in the master's program of the Department of Political Science. I sat in her Japanese language class, and we thus became friends. She became interested in Philippine politics, and at one time I accompanied her to the Malate Catholic School because she wanted to distribute questionnaires to high school students. She gave small tokens to the teachers who cooperated. When I went to Japan under the Japanese government scholarship, Yoko was back in Kyoto. I had been in Japan only a month when my father died. Yoko came all the way to Tokyo from Kyoto to keep me company and bring me to the airport when I left for Manila to attend my father's funeral. Yoko pursued her interest in Philippine politics and is now one of the Japanese authorities on the subject.

One of the instructors of Japanese language who came after Yoko left was Yokobayashi Hisayo. I often went out with her, visiting tourist spots in the Philippines or just eating out. I met Hisayo again in Sophia University when I was doing my doctoral studies. I had to read old, difficult, handwritten Japanese documents, and Hisayo was patient enough to sit with me and decipher those archaic characters not even my Japanese classmates could read.

Nakano Keiko, another instructor of Japanese language from ICU was a gourmet. She discovered mango pie and Magnolia ice cream and would bring them to Japan every time she had a chance. She introduced her whole family and lots of friends to Filipino fruits and cuisine. It was a two-way exchange because she would also bring all sorts of Japanese goodies and fruits to her Filipino friends every time she would visit, even after her term as visiting instructor of Japanese language had ended. She also loved native crafts—all the Japanese visiting professors loved native crafts—but Nakano-san was the one who would wear native earrings, necklaces, and bangles with pride. She was the type described in Japanese as "kao ga hiroi" (very sociable, with many friends and acquaintances). Whether in Japan or in the Philippines, she was "kao ga hiroi."

FINALLY, SUCCESS!

It was only in the 1980s that the economic power of Japan began to have an impact on cultural relations between Japan and the Philippines. As a result of the "hollowing out" of Japan, there was an increase in the number of Japanese companies that relocated to the Philippines. This meant job opportunities for those who had taken courses on Japan, especially for those who could speak even just basic Japanese. Filipino students finally warmed up to Japan. The number of Filipinos who wanted to study Japanese history, society, and culture began to increase. They wanted to discover the secret of Japan's economic success. The applicants to the annual competition for the Japanese government scholarship also began to increase. Naturally, students who had learned the Japanese language and/or subjects on Japan, showed more evidence of seriousness about studying in Japan than those who did not. This was certainly a motivation for students to take up Japan-related subjects and the Japanese language.

As a result of the favorable exchange value of the yen and the worsening economic conditions in the Philippines, Filipinos began to seek employment in Japan. This would have ripple effects on the Filipinos' image of, and interest in, Japan. Since there are many Filipinos in Japan, studying about Japan is no longer an irrelevant academic interest.

In November 1980, the thirteenth year of the program, the Ateneo president appointed from among its permanent senior faculty the first Filipino director of the Japanese Studies Program (Memo of

Jose A. Cruz, 1981). To the Japan Foundation, this was a good indication that Ateneo was still interested in maintaining the Japanese Studies Program.

By the mid-1980s the first Japanese Studies Program in the Philippines was a bona-fide program of the university. Its director and faculty were integral members of the university. In 1988 three A.B. courses (Communication, Economics, and Interdisciplinary Studies) and two B.S. (Management and Management Engineering) offered a minor in Japanese Studies, in coordination with the Japanese Studies Program. The minor in Japanese Studies was revised in 1991. Instead of other programs offering it to their students, the Japanese Studies Program played a more active role by offering it to all students, regardless of their majors. A minor in Japanese Studies became the first minor program in the Ateneo. Today, it is only one among the many minor programs, but it still has the most number of students, around thirty in the last two awarding of certificates ceremonies, March 2006 and 2007 (List of Students Minoring in Japanese Studies 2007). In 1998 the Japanese Studies Program launched a master's degree, major in Japanese Studies. So far, all its graduates are pursuing academic careers: three are doing doctoral studies in Japan, one has finished hers and is now a permanent faculty member of the University of the Philippines, the other is teaching in a Makati City university. The student who most recently finished his thesis is pursuing a law degree while teaching Japanese Language in the Japanese Studies Program. A short, revised version of his thesis is reproduced here (see Chapter 10).

The early establishment of the first Japanese Studies Program, the efforts of the Ateneo to retain it but not in the form that the Japan Foundation wanted, and the support that the Japan Foundation continued to give not in terms of salaries of visiting professors, but in other forms, such as book donations and support for specific projects, turned out to be wise decisions. When the demand for Japanese language and subjects about Japan increased in the 1990s, the Ateneo had the program to respond to it. It was not a fledgling program but one with a history of more than twenty years. In February 2007, the

Japanese Studies Program in the Ateneo turned forty years old, the most established Japanese Studies Program in the Philippines, and one of the oldest in Southeast Asia.

Notes

1. Professor here does not refer to a specific academic rank. It is a generic title usually used for teachers in institutions of higher learning in the Philippines, regardless of actual credentials.

2. In this essay, the age of the Japanese Studies Program in Ateneo is counted from its formal inauguration in 1967, and not from the opening of the first subjects taught under the program in December 1966.

3. The author, then enrolled in the Masters program of the Department of Political Science, took Japanese language in 1970 for free, and she had only three or four classmates.

4. That the International Christian University might not be able anymore to send professors to the Ateneo due to "lack of available personnel" was expressed in the Tentative Reassessment of the Japanese Program by Kasai Minoru, the incumbent director.

5. An issue the author had personal knowledge of was over the number of units the Japanese director of the program was supposed to teach. The director wanted to teach only three units, for that was the practice in Japan, according to him. In Ateneo, however, even the head of a department or a program would carry around nine teaching units in a semester.

References

(Unless otherwise stated, all documents are from the Ateneo de Manila University Archives.)

Announcement from the Dean of the College of Arts and Sciences of the Ateneo, Nicholas A. Kunkel. 1966. December 1.

Casual conversation with Dr. Benito Lim of the University of the Philippines, 2007 March.

Letter from Tadashi Inumaru, Executive Director of The Japan Foundation. 1974. September 10.

Letter of Bienvenido F. Nebres, Dean of the School of Arts and Sciences, the Ateneo, to Masaharu Yamada, Head, Japanese Studies Division of the Japan Foundation. 1973. October 25.

Letter of Bienvenido F. Nebres to Masaharu Yamada. 1974. June 14.

Letter to Mari-Jo P. Ruiz, Dean, School of Arts and Sciences. 1995.

List of Students Minoring in Japanese Studies. 2007. Japanese Studies Program Office.

Memo of John F. Doherty, Academic-Vice-President, to the Father Rector of the Ateneo. 1966 July 5.

Memo of Bienvenido F. Nebres, Dean, School of Arts and Sciences, the Ateneo, to Joseph Pittau and Michael Yanase. 1979. August 28.

Memo of Jose A. Cruz, President of the Ateneo, to the university community. 1981. February 6.

Memo to all units and department heads of the Ateneo from the Vice-President for Academic Affairs, John F. Doherty. [1966]. [December].

Memorandum from the JSP (Japanese Studies Program). [1966] [December].

Ministry of Justice homepage (moj.go.jp/PRESS/010613-1/010613-1-3. html) for 2000, viewed 2001 October 1.

Report of the Director [Haruo Tsuru] of the JSP. 1969.

Report of the Director [Haruo Tsuru)] of the JSP. 1971. December.

RP Official Gazette. 1948. 44, 1 (January).

Chapter 5

Networking through the Japan Society for the Promotion of Science: A Personal Account

Mari-Jo P. Ruiz

The Japan Society for the Promotion of Science (JSPS) exchange program between Japan and the Philippines was established to promote research in the basic sciences in the Philippines through sponsored interaction among Japanese and Filipino scientists. The program lasted for twenty years, from 1979 to 2000. The interaction took various forms: scientist exchange (from 1981), seminars (from 1990), and cooperative research (from 1993). The exchange was first established in the area of mathematics and was later extended to physics, chemistry and biology. It has had a tremendous impact on the development of the Philippine science community.

Brief History

It was in 1977 when the idea of the exchange began to take root. Professor Kawada Yukiyoshi of Sophia University had been very interested in promoting research in Asia, having been a member of the Commission for Development and Exchange of the International Mathematical Union (IMU). He invited the president of the Southeast Asian Mathematical Society (SEAMS) to a meeting in Tokyo to discuss the matter.

SEAMS is a group of mathematical societies of the countries in Southeast Asia. Founded in 1972, it included, at that time, the mathematical societies of Hongkong, Indonesia, Malaysia, the Philippines, Singapore and Thailand. Today, it also includes the mathematical societies of Brunei and Vietnam.

During the 1977 visit, Kawada and Fr. Bienvenido Nebres, S.J., president of SEAMS, initiated discussions with JSPS on the possibility of an exchange program between Japan and the Philippines. The initiative came at a time when JSPS was open to establishing regional exchanges. Exchange visits between scientists and officials of JSPS and their counterparts from the National Science Development Board of the Philippines (NSDB) culminated in a Memorandum of Understanding for Science Cooperation, which was signed in 1979.

The JSPS-NSDB exchange program in the basic sciences began at a time when the Consortium between three major Philippine universities—the University of the Philippines (UP), Ateneo de Manila University (ADMU), and De La Salle University (DLSU), was developing Ph.D. programs in the basic sciences. NSDB (which eventually became the National Science and Technology Agency or NSTA) and the Department of Science and Technology (DOST) were committed to support these programs, and therefore, the Consortium Ph.D. Programs became the beneficiaries of the exchange.

The Consortium was established to create core groups of science researchers in the country. The first Ph.D. program was in mathematics. The first batch of students graduated in 1980. Since there were less than five Ph.D.s in mathematics in the country at the time, the program was designed as a "sandwich program," i.e., students would take courses in the Philippines, start their dissertation with advisers from abroad, and return to the country to continue and complete research under the guidance of local advisers. The JSPS exchange was crucial in terms of providing visiting professors for the Ph.D. program, research opportunities for faculty members and dissertation advisers for Ph.D. students, although other countries like Australia,

China, France, Germany and Singapore were also supporting the Consortium Ph.D. program.

A measure of the success of the Ph.D. program in mathematics is the fact that from less than five in 1977, the country now has close to a hundred Ph.D.s in mathematics.

Prof. Shiga Koji was the first Japanese mathematician to visit the Philippines under the exchange program. His dedication and personal attention were crucial for the early stages of the exchange. Shiga chose prominent Japanese mathematicians and convinced them to come to the Philippines. Initially, they came to give lectures in the consortium Ph.D. program. Later, they came to do collaborative research with Filipino mathematicians.

In 1987 the management of the JSPS exchange between Japan and the Philippines shifted to the core university model. Sophia University served as the core university in Japan, while the UP-ADMU-DLSU Consortium served as the "core university" in the Philippines. With this change, Sophia took charge of organizing the participation of scientists from cooperating Japanese universities. The Consortium did the same in the Philippines.

Prof. Morimoto Mitsuo of Sophia University (currently academic vice-president of International Christian University) became the program coordinator for mathematics in 1987 and eventually the coordinator of the entire exchange in 1992. Morimoto's boundless enthusiasm and energy for the job was infectious. He was warmly received by Filipino mathematicians. He developed personal friendships with many of them and spurred the interest in research in analysis. Sophia professors Shinoda Ken-ichi, Yokonuma Takeo and Uchiyama Koichi continued the tradition of dedicated leadership and maintained the cordial nature of the mathematics exchange.

As the exchange progressed, research networks in graph theory, analysis and algebraic combinatorics emerged. Networks are not formal groupings but consist of a set of people who either do joint research, get together to discuss topics of common interest or organize conferences. I was part of the graph-theory network.

The Graph-Theory Network: Publications and Conferences

The initial links formed through JSPS were strengthened through other activities with Japanese mathematicians outside of JSPS. I was involved in the conceptualization and establishment of the journal *Graphs and Combinatorics* with Professors Akiyama Jin, Kano Mikio, Enomoto Hikoe and other Asian graph theorists. It was to be one of the first international mathematics journals originating from Asia. Springer-Verlag started publication in 1985. Today, *Graph and Combinatorics* is a prestigious ISI listed journal. I have been a member of the editorial board from the start. Akiyama is the current editor-in-chief, and Kano the managing editor.

Several Filipino mathematicians were invited to present papers at the First Japan Graph Theory Conference in Hakone in 1986. This conference expanded our horizons. The most important graph theorists in the world attended this conference. Our papers were well received and were published in reputable international journals, and we soon got invitations to other graph-theory conferences in the region such as those in China and Taiwan, and in other countries such as the US and France, in addition to our commitment to participate in the Southeast Asian Conferences.

By 1990 the JSPS exchange had expanded to include seminars. The first was the JSPS Seminar in Graph Theory held at Sophia University in August 1990. The refereed proceedings, edited by Akiyama and myself, were published. In the same year, 1990, the Second Japan Graph Theory Conference was held in Hakone. Nine Filipinos presented papers at this conference.

By 1991, the Filipino graph theorists had enough confidence to organize an international conference, Graph Theory and Combinatorics. This was a prestigious conference, attended by many graph-theory luminaries led by Claude Berge and Vasek Chvatal. Although this was not a JSPS-sponsored conference, it was strongly supported by many Japanese colleagues whom we met through the

JSPS exchange, as well as by colleagues from SEAMS. The proceedings of the conference were published as a special issue of the journal *Discrete Mathematics*. (Vol. 151, Nos. 1–3), edited by Norman Quimpo, a colleague in Ateneo de Manila, and myself.

From 1983 to 2000, approximately thirty-five papers, written either singly or jointly by members of the graph-theory network, were published in local, regional, and international journals and refereed conference proceedings. Papers written jointly by Japanese and Filipino members of the network continue to appear in international journals, the latest published in 2006.

Other Developments

The JSPS contacts made it possible for five young Filipinos to obtain doctoral degrees in mathematics at Japanese universities through Japanese Government Scholarship (popularly known then as Mombusho) grants from 1989 to 2004. Mathematicians who had been involved in some way with JSPS agreed to be the Ph.D. mentors of these students. This development formed linkages between a new generation of Filipino and Japanese mathematicians.

Success Factors and Measures

From 1987 to 2000, a total of fifty-two short-term visits were made by Filipino mathematicians to Japan while Japanese mathematicians made sixty-one visits to the Philippines. The list of publications arising from the exchange and the volumes of lecture notes published since 1984, the networks formed, the conferences organized, the working relationships and personal friendships that developed, the joint work between Filipino and Japanese mathematicians that continues by way of papers, projects and conferences—all these attest to the success of the exchange. The records show similar success stories in the other areas served by the exchange—Biology, Chemistry, and Physics.

The Filipino mathematicians who participated in the exchange all returned to academe as experienced researchers, to the benefit of mathematics education in the country. At present they not only teach mathematics but also contribute to the international effort to create new mathematics. They bring this newfound creativity to their classrooms and begin to build a research culture for the next generation.

Among the factors that contributed to the success of the mathematics exchange, I would include the following:

1. The vision and personal care of those who administered the exchange at the start.
2. The judicious choice of participants from both countries—the established Japanese professors, the mature and focused Filipino mathematicians.
3. The convergence of the goals of the JSPS Exchange Program and the UP-ADMU-DLSU Consortium.
4. The personal interest of the participants—their openness to working in a different culture and their appreciation of that culture.

Although the JSPS exchange has officially ended, the interaction between Japanese and Filipino mathematicians continues. This is a strong indicator that the objectives of the exchange have been achieved.

The graph-theory network and the algebraic combinatorics network came together for the Conference on Algebra and Combinatorics in March 2006. The comments from Japanese participants at that conference show that the exchange has remained faithful to the vision of Kawada. Mathematics cooperation began, survived and continues to flourish with friendship. Shinoda, commenting on the conference itself said: "I realize that this conference is all about love and friendship." Akiyama, commenting on long-term interaction said: "I learned . . . not only mathematics, but life—kindness, faithfulness, and above all, care for others."

References

Report of JSPS Core University Program with DOST in Breeder Sciences, April 1987–March 2000.

DOST-JSPS Joint Scientific Cooperation Program in the Breeder Sciences, 1979–1999, End Report.

Status Reports DOST-JSPS Exchange Program 1993–2000.

JSPS-DOST Scientific Cooperation Programs Participant Reports.

Personal communication from Jose Marasigan, Norman Quimpo, and Severino Gervacio.

The Philippine Airlines Basketball Team played with the basketball teams of several companies and universities in Japan in 1952. The matches were organized by the Japan Basketball Association, sponsored by the Yomiuri Newspaper, with the cooperation of the Ministry of Foreign Affairs and the Ministry of Education of Japan, and the Firipin Tomo no Kai, identified in the photo as "Friends of Philippines Society." (Photo credit: Firipin Kyokai)

Murata Shozo, head of the first Japanese goodwill mission to the Philippines, presents gifts to Philippine President Ramon Magsaysay (standing, third from Murata), 9 August 1956. (Photo credit: Firipin Kyokai)

President Carlos P. Garcia addresses the Japanese Diet (Parliament), the first foreigner to be given the honor, 2 December 1958. (Photo credit: Firipin Kyokai)

President Diosdado Macapagal, assisted by ECAFE (Economic Commission for Asia and the Far East) Executive Secretary U Nyun, unveils the Asian Development Bank (ADB) marker in its former office in Pasay City, 3 December 1965. Behind the president is the First Lady Eva Macapagal. Before occupying this office, ADB was temporarily housed in the Metrobank Building in Makati. ADB is now located in the modern commercial area of Ortigas, Pasig. (Reprinted with permission from ADB: www.adb.org.)

The Japanese Garden in Luneta Park (Rizal Park) was inaugurated on 11 June 1969 with Philippine President Ferdinand Marcos, the First Lady Imelda Marcos and former prime minister of Japan Kishi Nobusuke as guests of honor. The following year, 1970 August, this marker was installed. (Photo credit: Firipin Kyokai)

Relic of the past: This concrete structure, called tochika (fortification), stands at the foot of Sigue Bridge in the outskirts of Iloilo City. It was used by the Japanese as watch post during World War II. Today, it is a convenient signpost, aside from being a source of curiosity among passersby. (Photo credit: LYJ)

Ambassador of the Philippines to Japan, Ramon del Rosario (second from left), is given a welcome party by the Firipin Kyokai (Philippine Society in Japan), 10 July 1986, months after the People Power Revolution that toppled the Marcos dictatorship and the ascendancy of Corazon Aquino to the presidency. Former Prime Minister Fukuda Takeo delivers a speech. To the left of Fukuda is Benjamin Sanvictores, Deputy Chief of Missions. Sanvictores was a Japanese government pensionado during World War II. (Photo credit: Firipin Kyokai)

Ikebana demonstration at the hall of the Japan Information and Cultural Center (JICC), 1968. (Photo credit: Cecilia P. Tolentino)

A montage of photos and origami (Japanese art of paper folding) with labels in Japanese: The photo on the left shows a volunteer of the Intercommunication Center for Asia and Nippon (ICAN), a Japanese NGO, with three children of Payatas. In NGO work of development and poverty alleviation, there is space for imparting culture. (Photo credit: Junefe Payot)

Near the Manila Cathedral in Intramuros, stands this memorial to the civilian victims of the liberation of Manila in 1945. The stone sculpture depicting the grieving Mary, Mother of God in the Catholic belief, was commissioned by the relatives and friends of those who died. The relatives and friends have formed an association, Memorare – Manila 1945, Incorporated, the main purpose of which is to keep alive the memory of the civilian victims of the war. (Photo credit: LYJ)

The "Goddess of Mercy and Virgin of Pilgrims for Peace," depicted in a Buddhist way stand along the road to the Dambana ng Kagitingan (Shrine of Valor), Mount Samat, Bataan. This is one way by which the Japanese memorialize their war dead. (Photo credit: LYJ)

Chapter 6

Emerging Asia—Partnership between the Philippines and Japan through the Asian Development Bank*

Senga Kunio and Alely Alejar-Bernardo

THIS CHAPTER REVIEWS THE SOCIOECONOMIC PARTNERSHIP BETWEEN the Philippines and Japan through the operations of the Asian Development Bank (ADB) in a dynamic and rapidly changing Asia and Pacific region.

It consists of five parts. The first part provides a brief overview of the ADB and its operations while the second part describes the role Japan plays in ADB. The third part elaborates on the existing partnership that ADB has with the Philippines, followed by part four, which describes and illustrates how Japan supports Philippine development through the ADB. And finally, the last part touches on key issues and challenges in Asia and the Philippines and presents how ADB, with the help of its development partners including Japan, is poised to address these issues and challenges.

Brief Overview of ADB and its Operations

The work of ADB is aimed at improving the welfare of the people in Asia and the Pacific, particularly the 1.9 billion who live on less than two dollars a day. Despite many success stories, the region remains home to two-thirds of the world's poor.

ADB is a multilateral regional development bank. "Multilateral" because it involves many countries, "regional" as it covers Asia and the Pacific region; "development" because it is concerned with economic growth and cooperation, and "bank" because it lends money.

ADB is a partnership of the developing countries of the region and the developed countries of the world. When ADB was established in 1966, it had thirty-one founding members, which included Japan and the Philippines. Today, ADB's membership has doubled, growing to sixty-six countries, of which forty-seven are from the Asian region which include the most populous countries in Asia and the tiniest island-states of the Pacific; and nineteen from outside the region which include most of the richest countries in North America and Europe. Its two newest member countries are Brunei and Ireland. The largest shareholders are Japan and the United States at about 13 percent shares each.

ADB is dedicated to reducing poverty in Asia and the Pacific region through pro-poor sustainable economic growth, social development, and good governance. With headquarters in Manila, ADB has twenty-six offices around the world and more than 2,000 staff members from over fifty countries.

Vision. ADB's vision is a region free of poverty. Its mission is to help its developing member countries (DMCs) reduce poverty and improve the quality of life of their citizens. ADB strongly supports the Millennium Development Goals (MDGs) which define specific goals and targets with indicators for measuring and monitoring progress toward poverty reduction. These goals provide an important basis for ADB's developing member countries to prepare their own poverty reduction strategies, in collaboration with development partners. These also help align ADB's assistance programs with country-specific needs and priorities.

Organization. ADB recently underwent a realignment of the regional departments' country groupings to enhance operational effectiveness by balancing portfolio sizes, improving regional departments' country focus, and strengthening the synergy between country and

Chart 1. ADB's Simplified Organizational Structure as of May 2006

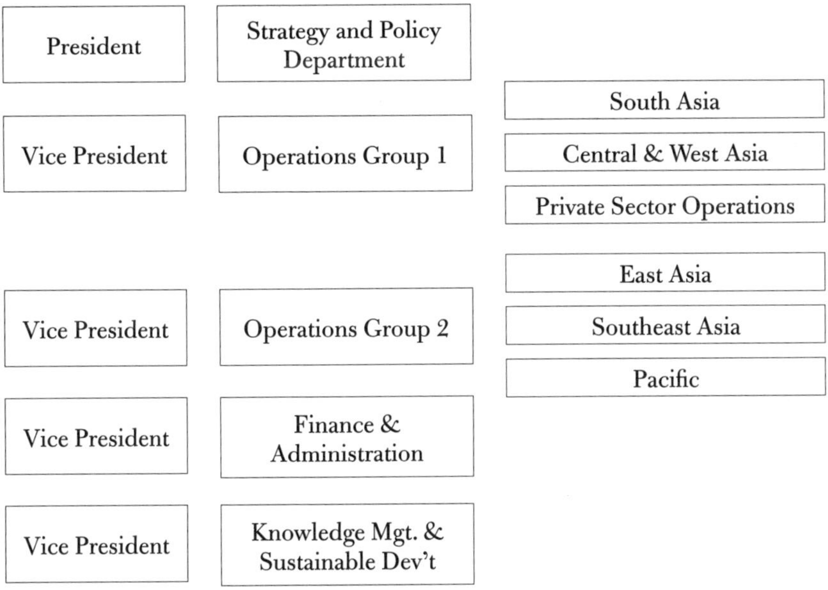

See Asian Development Bank website for the full organizational chart.

regional operations. The new organizational structure shows country operations being divided into two major groups covering private sector operations and the following regional departments, namely (i) South Asia, (ii) Central and West Asia, (iii) East Asia, (iv) Southeast Asia, and (v) the Pacific (Chart 1). ADB is headed by a president—always a Japanese national—assisted by four vice presidents.

Operations. ADB provides assistance mainly to governments for specific projects and programs. ADB's main instruments for providing help to its DMCs include (i) policy dialogue, (ii) loans, (iii) technical assistance (TA), (iv) grants, (v) guarantees, and (vi) equity investments.

ADB's annual lending volume is typically about $6 billion dollars, with TAs usually totaling about $180 million a year. In 2005, ADB operations totaled $7.4 billion in loans, equities, guarantees, grants, and TA (Table 1). Of this total amount, $5.8 billion went to seventy-two ADB-approved loans (sixty-four projects), $1.2 billion to fifty-one grant-financed projects and $198.7 million to 299 TA operations.

Table 1. ADB Operations, 2005

OPERATIONS	AMOUNT ($ million)		
Lending			5,796.8
Public		5,260.8	
of which: OCR	3,885.2		
ADF	1,375.6		
Private		536.0	
Equity and Guarantee			285.5
Grant-financed Projects			1,151.4
Technical Assistance			198.7
Total			7,432.4

By recipient country, the bulk of ADB's lending operations went to the People's Republic of China, Indonesia, Pakistan, Viet Nam and Bangladesh. By sector, a major share of lending operations went to transport and communications (30 percent), followed by energy (19 percent) and multisector (15 percent). It may also be noted that during this period, ADB responded with speed and flexibility to two major natural disasters that hit Asia, providing $850 million for the countries affected by the Indian Ocean tsunami, and $1 billion for Pakistan when it was hit by a crushing earthquake.

JAPAN'S ROLE IN THE ADB

As noted earlier, Japan is ADB's largest shareholder—coequally with the United States—in terms of capital contributions. In fact, Japan is the number-one partner overall as it is the top supporter of ADB's concessional loan window called Asian Development Fund (ADF) with almost 40 percent contributions. At the end of 2005, Japan's contribution to the ADF totaled $8.60 billion, accounting for 38.55

percent of the total ADF committed. Aside from Japan, the other large contributors are the United States, Canada, Germany, Australia, France, and the United Kingdom.

Japan also channels its financial support to ADB through a TA facility called Japan Special Fund and also through the ADB Institute. Japan's other financial contributions include support for (i) TA Special Fund (TASF), which provides grants to borrowing members to facilitate the flow and efficient use of development finance to DMCs and to enhance their development capacity; (ii) loan cofinancing, mainly through the Japan Bank for International Cooperation (JBIC) of large priority projects; and (iii) grant cofinancing.

Japan also has agreements with ADB to manage various trust funds which target specific activities. One of these is the Japan Fund for Poverty Reduction (JFPR) which supports poverty reduction and related social development activities that can add substantive value to ADB-financed projects. The JFPR's objectives are to (i) support well-targeted poverty reduction and social development activities that have a direct impact on the poor and on socially or economically excluded or vulnerable groups; (ii) stimulate the self-help capacities of the poor; (iii) stimulate widespread stakeholder participation at the community level; and (iv) provide a systematic impact on DMCs' operations and approaches toward sustainable poverty reduction.

ADB-Philippines Partnership

The Philippines' Role in the ADB. The Philippines has a special relationship with ADB, being the host country for its headquarters and supplying essential support for ADB to serve its other members. The Philippines is a founding member of ADB and the eleventh largest shareholder. Since 1969, ADB has been actively extending its support to development programs in the Philippines through lending and TA programs and projects. Since that time and up to December 2005, 195 loans amounting to $8.8 billion have been approved, along with 316 TA projects totaling $142 million. Cumulatively, the Philippines is ADB's fifth largest borrower and TA recipient, and ADB's largest client for approved private sector loan, equity investment, and guarantee operations.

In the wake of the 1997 financial crisis, ADB's new lending to the Philippines was constrained by a lack of fiscal space for investment spending. Tax revenues dropped sharply, and interest on debt consumed about one-third of the total budget spending in 2005. New lending was affected also by weak implementation of ADB's active loan portfolio, and a mismatch between ADB's loan products and the needs of a country (such as the Philippines) with access to international capital markets. Each of these issues has been addressed.

The active public loan portfolio has been dramatically transformed from one of ADB's weakest to one of the best, providing a platform for processing new projects. Similarly, the success of the Philippine government with fiscal consolidation has improved the opportunity for supporting ongoing and proposed projects. ADB has improved its relevance and responsiveness to ordinary capital resources (OCR) which includes the Philippines by introducing new lending products, widening the eligibility of expenditures that can be financed, and simplifying processing.

ADB's Vision for the Philippines. The Philippines suffers from a high incidence of poverty and income inequality. Among Asian countries, the Philippines has the sixth largest number of poor living on about one dollar a day. Thus, the cornerstone of the Philippine Medium Term Development Plan is "freedom from persistent, pervasive and intense poverty." As a development partner, ADB fully shares this aspiration and is committed to achieve this goal in coordination with other development partners. In that regard, ADB and the Philippines share a common vision, reflecting an important partnership.

ADB's Support for the Philippines. The ADB assistance strategy to the Philippines has evolved over the years. The principal driving force behind the evolution has been the readiness of ADB to adjust its strategy and programs to the changing circumstances of the country. In recent years, as the economy achieved some measure of stabilization, the Philippine government has increasingly shifted its priorities toward poverty reduction and social development. This shift has been accompanied by an increase in emphasis on environmental management, good governance, and capacity building, development themes that rank high in ADB priorities.

At present, ADB's support is embodied in the Philippine Country Strategy and Program (CSP), 2005–2007 which takes into account lessons from the partnership experience, covering upstream strategy formulation and programming, and downstream portfolio management and project implementation. It is informed by ADB's assistance assessments, the intensive portfolio cleanup of the past years, and economic and sector work.

The CSP also makes a significant break with the past. The strategy is more focused, emphasizing fiscal consolidation, an improved investment climate, and accelerated attainment of MDGs; and there is greater selectivity of projects to be supported. The partnership is aligned with the Philippines' own strategic priorities and uses a results framework with more attention to outcomes and impact than inputs and outputs. ADB's assistance covers all major social and economic sectors, such as agriculture, natural resources, energy, transport, and social infrastructure (Table 2). Policy dialogue and reform measures conducted in association with the lending and TA activities have helped the Philippines and other development partners address constraints to development and problems affecting timely implementation of development projects, and have built required institutional and implementation capacity for the Philippines' project management and project implementation agencies.

To date, there are twenty-six ongoing projects. ADB's support and assistance to the ongoing projects include (i) policy and technical support to ensure timely project implementation, improvement of financial management and procurement operations; (ii) harmonization of operational activities for project implementation and project management between the Philippines and major donor agencies; (iii) streamlining of the project implementation process and procedures

Table 2. Philippines: Cumulative ADB Lending by Sector (as of 31 December 2005)

SECTOR	LOANS (No.)	AMOUNT ($ million)	%
Energy	27	2,283.6	26.0
Agriculture and natural resources	46	1,538.5	17.5
Multisector	28	1,175.8	13.4
Finance	21	1,166.0	13.3
Transport and communications	26	1,105.9	12.6
Water supply, sanitation and waste management	20	731.1	8.3
Health, nutrition and social protection	6	317.4	3.6
Education	8	252.1	2.9
Industry and trade	12	225.8	2.6
Law, economic management, and public policy	1	3.0	0.0
Total	**195**	**8,799.0**	**100.0**

*Totals may not add due to rounding

for local government units; and (iv) provision and sharing of information on major project implementation issues and portfolio performance monitoring and evaluation.

External Funding Coordination and Partnership Arrangements. ADB's financial and technical resources complement those from development partners, under the paradigm of "moving from coordination to cooperation." The range of development partners is widening to include more intensive dialogue with civil society, members of Congress, and the private sector. In conjunction with its lending program, ADB continues to pursue cofinancing from other official and commercial sources, and private sector partners.

ADB is working with the Philippines and other development partners on the commitments made under the Paris Declaration on Aid Effectiveness. For instance, joint missions with the World Bank, JBIC, and some other bilateral partners maintain a consistent dialogue on harmonization and adoption of country systems. ADB also cooperates extensively with civil society organizations in the Philippines to strengthen the effectiveness, quality, and sustainability of the services it provides.

Turning to a broader form of partnership, how do other donor partners, in particular Japan, assist Philippine development through the ADB?

JAPAN'S SUPPORT FOR PHILIPPINE DEVELOPMENT THROUGH ADB

Japan's Assistance to the Philippines. Japan has remained the top donor in the Philippines for the past two decades (Embassy of Japan in the Philippines website). The Philippines has been receiving Japanese assistance to support various development activities through (i) bilateral grants (i.e., grant aid and technical cooperation) and ODA loans; and (ii) multilateral ODA which refers to contributions and subscriptions to multilateral institutions such as the ADB, World Bank, and various United Nations agencies.

Along with the growth of Japan's bilateral ODA in recent years, the international community has increasingly called for Japan to play a more active leadership role in multilateral institutions. Consequently, for the Philippines and other developing countries in Asia and the Pacific region, Japan attaches growing importance to aid provided through the ADB.

ADB-Japan cooperation and coordination in the Philippines. In order to maximize their development impact, Japan and the ADB cooperates in several areas that encompass (i) policy advocacy, (ii) project-related activities, including TA, (iii) human resources development; and (iv) other complementarities in area- and sector-specific activities. In support of key Government programs and policies, various formal and informal institutional platforms exist to provide strong communication and collaboration between the two partners.

Examples of how ADB and Japan are jointly pursuing these efforts in the country are elaborated further in the succeeding discussions.

Partner Coordination at the Policy Level. ADB-Japan cooperation and coordination in and with the Philippines covers policy dialogue among all development partners through the Philippines Development Forum (PDF). The PDF is the primary mechanism of the Philippines for facilitating substantive policy dialogue among stakeholders on the country's development agenda. It also serves as a process for developing consensus and generating commitments among different stakeholders toward critical actionable items of the Philippines' reform agenda.

The PDF has established seven thematic working groups (WG) which reflect the Forum's prioritization of development constraints. ADB and Japan are active participants in most of the groups. The WGs meet regularly to clarify issues and to develop prioritized reform agendas, with the aim of facilitating its contribution to the work of the country's economic management team. Each WG is led by a Government agency as lead convenor with a development partner as co-chair. Japan's International Finance Corporation is the development partner co-lead convenor with the Department of Finance on the WG on economic and fiscal reform. On the other hand, the ADB is the co-lead convenor with the Office of the Ombudsman for the WG on governance and anti-corruption. ADB also leads in policy dialogue for the power sector and capital market reforms.

In addition, ADB and Japan work closely through regular technical working group meetings as well as joint studies that examine and inform their future strategies and programs, such as the recent study on infrastructure which was also conducted jointly with the World Bank.

Partnership at the Project Level. ADB actively seeks cofinancing partners for TAs and loans to reduce the burden of project financing on the Philippine Government budget. Japan is an active partner in ADB in the provision of these additional resources for project financing to support important projects in such sectors as transport, water,

Table 3. Philippines: ADB Projects Cofinanced with Japan, 1995-2005 (Amounts in US$ million)

Project (Year Approved)	ADB Loan Amount	Japan Project Cofinancing Amount
Electricity Market and Transmission Development (2002)	40.00	40.00
North Luzon Expressway Rehabilitation & Expansion (2000)	45.00	10.71
Power Sector Restructuring Program (1998)	300.00	300.00
Secondary Education Development & Improvement Program (1998)	53.00	54.30
Metro Manila Air Quality Improvement Program (1998)	271.00	300.00
Power Transmission Reinforcement (1997)	191.40	7.50
Fisheries Resource Management (1997)	20.22	19.30
Sixth Road Project (1996)	167.00	160.00
Northern Luzon Transmission and Generation (1995)	180.00	244.00
Total	**1,267.62**	**835.81**

education, environment and natural resources (including forestry and fisheries).

Over the past ten years, Japan has provided cofinancing for several projects in the Philippines totaling US$835.81 million (Table 3). Aside from JBIC's non-ODA window, Japanese private firms like Sumitomo Mitsui and Dai-ichi Kangyo banks have been important sources of cofinancing for these projects.

One of the ongoing ADB projects cofinanced by Japan is the Metro Manila Air Quality Improvement Program, which aims to provide resources to implement an Air Quality Action Plan to tackle deteriorating air quality in the Metro Manila air shed. The Program further aims to promote policy reforms to improve air quality through

Table 4. Philippines: ADB-approved JFPR Grant Proposals (as of 31 May 2006; Amounts in US$ million)

APPROVED JFPR GRANT PROJECTS	JFPR GRANT AMOUNT
Strategic Private Sector Partnerships for Urban Poverty Reduction in Metro Manila (STEP-UP)	3.60
Supporting the Sustainable Livelihood for the Poor in Southern Philippines	2.80
Renewable Energy and Livelihood Development for the Poor in Negros Occidental	1.50
Social Protection for Poor Women Vendors in Mindanao Cities	1.00
Off-Site and Off-City Relocation of Vulnerable Slum Communities of Muntinlupa City	1.00
On-Site Urban Upgrading for Vulnerable Slum Communities of Payatas	1.00
Developing Financial Cooperatives	0.90
Total	**11.80**

the abatement of main mobile and stationary sources of air pollution. The loan supports public sector investments for traffic engineering and management, traffic enforcement capacity, training in traffic planning and management, road rehabilitation, ambient air quality monitoring facilities, antismoke-belching programs, capacity building and institutional development, training for air quality management, and consulting services. At present, the Program is being jointly implemented by the Metro Manila Development Authority, and the Departments of Public Highways, Transport and Communications, and Environment and Natural Resources.

Last but not the least, the JFPR directly supports poverty reduction and related social development activities that add substantive value to ADB-financed projects in the country. To date, a total of seven JFPR grant proposals have been approved by the Government of

Japan concerning urban poverty and social protection, among other Philippine development activities (Table 4).

One of the notable projects is the Strategic Private Sector Partnerships for Urban Poverty Reduction in Metro Manila (STEP-UP) which targets twenty-three poor communities in Metro Manila, or about 35,000 people, of whom 60 percent are severely poor. The project has three components, namely (i) strategic partnership building; (ii) funds for housing improvement, livelihood, and community infrastructure; and (iii) risk reduction and management.

Another JFPR project, involving the provision of renewable energy and livelihood development for the poor in Negros Occidental, is a good example of ADB-Japan partnership in the Philippines.

Meanwhile, in order to ensure a more manageable portfolio and successful project implementation, ADB and JBIC, along with the World Bank, work closely through joint portfolio reviews. These joint efforts have led to remarkable improvements in project implementation performance indicators, including a significant reduction in undisbursed loans, and in the proportion of project "at risk."

Cooperation on Other Project Grants and Technical Assistance. As earlier noted, Japan channels its support through ADB under special funds for which the Philippines has been one of the major beneficiaries. These special funds (also called trust funds) are administered by ADB on behalf of the Japanese Government:

- The Japan Special Fund (JSF) supports activities related to environment protection, gender and development, private sector promotion, and finance sector reform. Since the Fund's establishment in ADB in 1988, the Philippines has received ninety TAs amounting to $56.0 million. In 2005, the Philippines benefited from an advisory TA on microfinance development.
- Japan also responded to the Philippines' needs during the Asian Financial Crisis through the Asian Currency Crisis Special Fund (ACCSF). During the period 1999–2002, the Philippines received ten advisory and project preparatory TAs amounting to $9.5

million to support various efforts ranging from strengthening of technical education to anti-money laundering.

- Japan also provides a facility for information and communication technology (ICT) through the Japan Fund for ICT (JFICT) which is currently supporting the development of the Philippine business registry. Just recently, the Philippines received another JFICT grant amounting to US$500,000 to help provide more efficient and effective public services in the country.

Joint Support for Human Resources Development. The ADB-Japan Scholarship Program (JSP) was established in 1988 to provide opportunities for qualified individuals from ADB's DMCs to pursue postgraduate studies in economics, management, science and technology, and other development-related fields at twenty educational institutions in ten countries in Asia and the Pacific. Through ADB, close to 2,000 students have been awarded scholarships under the JSP. The Philippines has had one of the highest numbers of recipients, with 160 scholars, or 8 percent of the total, as of the end of 2005. The Philippines ranks fourth in terms of the number of JSP awardees.

Complementarities in Other Area- and Sector-Specific Activities. Taking into consideration their respective comparative advantages, ADB and Japan cooperate and coordinate their respective forms of assistance in various sectors such as agriculture and rural development, agrarian reform, energy, transport, health, water supply and sanitation, governance and finance, and gender and development.

For instance, in the education sector, ADB's assistance aims to strengthen policy reforms, build capacity and provide quality improvement in basic education, higher education and skills training. On the other hand, JBIC helps in improving quality and access to primary and secondary education, and provides cofinancing for ADB and WB secondary and elementary education projects. The Japan International Cooperation Agency (JICA) helps in improving primary and secondary education; supports physical infrastructure development such as school buildings, classrooms and teaching equipment; supports science and mathematics education; and provides teaching materials/equipment.

In the environment and natural resources management sectors, ADB supports environmental management by improving the environmental quality of urban centers, as well as by supporting improvements in managing solid and medical waste. ADB, likewise, helps protect and manage natural resources by (i) supporting the use of a community-based, demand-driven participatory approach to prevent deforestation and degradation of forestland; and (ii) promoting sustainable and integrated management of coastal resources and related ecosystems. On the other hand, JBIC funds air quality improvement programs, in partnership with ADB, and supports community-based forestry management, fisheries and coastal resources management. Meanwhile, JICA provides environmental management capacity building, and supports mining, pollution prevention, solid waste management, and forest conservation.

ADB has co-led, with JBIC and the World Bank, harmonization of procurement and financial management policies and procedures in the Philippines, which is a strong supporter of the effort to reduce transactions costs of dealing with development partners, and is a pilot for country-level harmonization under the global harmonization effort. The foregoing examples clearly illustrate how the ADB and Japan have nurtured an active partnership in the Philippines.

ISSUES AND CHALLENGES IN DEVELOPING ASIA AND THE PHILIPPINES

Asian Economic Performance and Outlook. In 2005, aggregate gross domestic product for the Asian region expanded by a robust 7.4 percent. Growth was underpinned by a favorable external environment and by continuing progress in domestic reform issues. In Southeast Asia, there was notable performance in Indonesia and accelerated growth in Cambodia, Viet Nam and Laos, but slower pace of growth in Malaysia, Thailand, the Philippines and Singapore.

ADB's Asian Development Outlook (ADO) 2006 notes that Asia is well positioned for sustained growth over the medium term. The region is favored by geography, demographics, and the conviction among leading policymakers that integration with the global economy will strengthen the region. The profile of risks facing developing Asia remains much as before, but these risks are probably more accentuated. A jump of the avian flu to people, yet higher oil prices, a disorderly unraveling of global payment imbalances, or a surge in trade protectionism would unsettle the outlook.

Asia is changing. Yet there remain immense challenges, among them:

Persistent poverty despite high growth. Some 620 million Asians, two-thirds of the world's poor people, still live on less than a dollar a day. In addition, disparities between Asian countries have increased significantly since the 1990s. While the region is broadly on track for achieving the MDGs for reducing income poverty, it is less so for non-income dimensions of poverty such as children's undernutrition, net primary enrollment rate, and reduction of infant and maternal mortality.

Poor investment climate. The region's high growth is at risk because of its poor investment climate. The region's overall investment rate (25 percent) may not be enough to sustain a regional growth rate of 6 percent. Some estimates indicate a deficit of $200 billion annually for infrastructure investment in East Asia alone.

Governance remains weak. There is a high incidence of corruption in many DMCs. Corruption, inefficiency, and poor capacity in public systems not only impede investment but also add large transaction costs to ongoing private economic activities, reduce the quality of life, and weaken public social and economic programs, eroding the effectiveness of DMCs' development efforts.

Environmental degradation. High growth has concomitant environmental costs. Demographic pressure and growth are driving rapid urbanization, with 36 percent of Asians now living in urban areas, and as many as eleven megacities each supporting over ten-million people. Moreover, the region faces the challenge of natural disasters.

Issues and Challenges Facing the Philippines. Current growth rates in the Philippines are not enough to significantly reduce unemployment, underemployment and poverty. For the past decade, the Philippines has been growing at about 2 percent, or less than half of other ASEAN countries—Indonesia, Malaysia, Thailand, and Singapore. At this rate, while these neighboring countries will take sixteen years for their GDP per capita to double, the Philippines will take thirty-five years.

In 2005 economic growth slowed to 5.1 percent in 2005 and inflation accelerated to 7.6 percent. Introduction of the expanded value-added tax helped lift confidence in the outlook at a time of political uncertainty, though the quality of fiscal consolidation will be watched closely. Investment continues to lag, while the dependence of growth on consumption and on remittance inflows limits prospects (Asian Development Outlook 2006, 214–19).

The Philippines has plenty of "catching up" to do, based on the outlook that over the near term, growth in the Philippines is expected to stay largely unchanged. Thus, the key challenge for the Philippines is to reignite investment demand and to ensure that domestic savings are put to good use. Other key challenges for the country include the government's ability to address reforms in the fiscal sector (i.e., tax administration, revenue and customs collections, etc.). Reforms in the power sector likewise need to be facilitated and sustained.

Given these key issues and challenges in Asia and the Philippines, how is ADB posed to address these issues and challenges, in active partnership with the country's stakeholders, especially Japan?

ADB's Medium Term Strategy. With support from Japan, ADB recently adopted its Second Medium Term Strategy, or MTS II, in May 2006. The strategic priorities and business model adjustments of MTS II will further strengthen the poverty reduction impact of ADB's operations and enable ADB to be more relevant, responsive and effective in the changing context of the Asian region and the Philippines.

The implementation of MTS will be country-focused and will be operationalized through individual country strategy and program documents that will be consolidated in ADB's Work Program and Budget Framework. Thus, several changes are expected in ADB's operations resulting from the implementation of MTS II, and will benefit the Philippines, both at the strategic and operational levels.

ADB's Continued Engagement with Middle-Income Countries (MICs), including the Philippines. ADB recognizes that the needs and expectations of MICs are now much more varied and different from the past. ADB, together with its other development partners, is developing new approaches that are both responsive to the needs and demands of MICs and are more sharply focused on achieving measurable results.

To maximize the contribution it can make, ADB recently issued a paper, entitled "Enhancing Asian Development Bank Support to Middle-Income Countries and Borrowers from Ordinary Capital Resources" (Asian Development Bank website) to provide a coherent framework for the various measures being undertaken or considered to enhance support to OCR borrowers. These measures can be grouped into the following broad areas, namely (i) reducing the costs of doing business with ADB; (ii) enhancing and expanding the range of instruments; and (iii) enhancing service quality.

Among other principles, the MIC strategy calls for stronger donor collaboration—both through the provision of financial resources and TA in these countries. Through increased collaboration, ADB can leverage the impact of assistance in support of MDGs, infrastructure and regional public goods. In this regard, ADB-Japan partnership in the Philippines will be increasingly relevant.

ADB's Innovation and Efficiency Initiatives (IEI). The IEI, begun in 2003, was designed to streamline business processes, reduce transaction costs and processing time, and develop and pilot-test new instruments and modalities. Several measures have already been adopted under the IEI and are expected to benefit the Philippines.

ADB's Support for Regional Cooperation and Integration (RCI). At the beginning of the year, ADB's President noted that "the movement toward a more integrated East Asian economy offers important opportunities to the Philippines at a time when there is urgent need to build on progress in macroeconomic stabilization and move to a path of sustained strong growth" (Kuroda 2006). He further outlined the steps needed to ensure that Philippine businesses and workers can compete successfully in the regional and global markets, and restore the confidence needed to make the Philippines an active player in the Asian integration process.

As the Philippines moves ahead in RCI efforts, ADB can help in many ways, *viz*:

- Providing direct support for the domestic reform and competitiveness agenda. As pointed out earlier, ADB's Philippine CSP focuses on fiscal consolidation, on improvements in the investment climate, and on improved governance. Technical assistance and lending operations are under way or under preparation to support the restructuring of key government owned and controlled corporations, particularly in the critical energy sector.
- Providing support for regional cooperation in Southeast Asia, under the new Regional Cooperation Strategy and Program, which focuses on transport and energy infrastructure development, along with support for joint efforts to improve marine resource management in the Sulu/Sulawesi Sea region, facilitate trade, and promote enhanced and harmonized port security.
- Providing support for BIMP-EAGA (the Brunei Darussalam-Indonesia-Malaysia-Philippines East ASEAN Growth Area), a regional initiative in which the Philippines participates, that has already received considerable ADB technical assistance.
- Supporting the other regional programs in which the Philippines participates, including the ASEAN and ASEAN+3 and the Asian Bond Markets Initiative.

Note

* The views and opinions of authors expressed in this paper do not necessarily state or reflect those of the Asian Development Bank (ADB). The authors

wish to acknowledge the inputs provided by Mr. Koide Haruya, Principal Regional Cooperation and Infrastructure Financing Specialist, Operations Coordination Division, South Asia Department, ADB. The assistance of the ADB Philippine Country Office headed by Country Director Thomas Crouch is likewise gratefully acknowledged.

References

Asian Development Bank website. http://www.adb.org

Asian Development Bank. 2005. *Philippine Country Strategy and Program, 2005–2007.*

_____. *Asian Development Outlook 2006.* June.

_____. 2006. *ADB Second Medium Term Strategy, 2006–2008.* May.

_____. 2003. *Country Assistance Program Evaluation in the Philippines.* January.

_____. 2006. *ADB's Regional Cooperation and Integration Strategy.* ADB Strategy Paper. July.

_____. 2006. *Enhancing Asian Development Bank Support to Middle-Income Countries and Borrowers from Ordinary Capital Resources.* ADB Strategy Paper. August.

ADB-World Bank-Japan Bank for International Cooperation (ADB-WB-JBIC). 2005. *Connecting East Asia: A New Framework for Infrastructure.* Joint ADB-WB-JBIC Study.

Embassy of Japan in the Philippines website. http://www.ph.emb-japan.go.jp

Kuroda Haruhiko. 2006. *Asian Economic Integration: Opportunities for Philippine Development.* Speech delivered at The Asia Society Philippine Forum, 17 January Peninsula Manila Hotel, Manila.

Chapter 7

At the Core of Filipina-Japanese Intercultural Marriages: Family, Gender, Love and Cross-Cultural Understanding

Satake Masaaki

Japanese are ambivalent over the "multiculturalization" of Japanese society. Some insist on the preservation of the assumed racial purity of Japan. Others deny the growing presence of foreigners. But the fact that Japan is host to 2 million foreigners, including Filipinas married to Japanese men, and that such marriages rank second among cross-cultural marriages, is undeniable.

This chapter focuses on the family orientation of Filipino wives and their Japanese husbands, as well as patterns of negotiations between them. On the domestic domain, affective relations and marital conflicts provide both space for engagement and negotiation of cultural differences. Filipino wives try to resolve marital conflicts in varied ways ranging from subtle to direct confrontation and stubborn persistence. Some Japanese husbands respond positively and in the process, compromise their male-oriented values and discard their traditional male-dominant orientations. The result is "male liberation."

On the other hand, as the chapter will show, in some cases of intercultural marriages, establishment of better relations with their Filipino wives is a result not merely of negotiation but primarily of the husbands' concern and affection for their wives.

Furthermore, the chapter will show that through varied cross-cultural experiences, both Filipino wives and Japanese husbands broaden their perspectives. An intercultural marriage is a potential venue where both partners can enrich their world-views depending on each one's values and ability to accommodate cultural differences.

This study is based on interviews with Filipino-Japanese couples in Kagawa and Tokushima prefectures, Shikoku, Western Japan, as well as those in Aichi Prefecture, Central Japan and in Sydney, Australia. The in-depth participant observation is a product of long-time encounters with various Filipino-Japanese couples between 1999 and 2007. Furthermore, the author organized focus group discussions among the Japanese husbands in 2004 and 2005. In addition, at the Sakura-machi Catholic Church in Takamatsu City, capital of Kagawa, the author distributed questionnaires to Filipino-Japanese couples and supplemented some of them with interviews.

OVERVIEW OF INTERCULTURAL MARRIAGES IN JAPAN

In 2005, out of 714,265 registered marriages in Japan, marriages between Japanese nationals and non-Japanese, which shall here be called intercultural marriages, numbered 41,481 (see Table 1). In Japan, such marriages are usually called k*okusai kekkon,* or "international marriages." But to avoid emphasis on the nation or the nation-state, and to highlight the cultural context of such unions, the author prefers to use the term "intercultural marriage" (Cahill 1990, 4–5). Such unions have surged, as compared to 25,626 in 1990 and 12,181 in 1985. Within the two decades since 1985, Japan's intercultural marriages have more than tripled.

Intercultural marriages constitute 5.81 percent of all the registered marriages in 2005. This translates to one intercultural marriage out of every twenty.

Intercultural marriages in Japan are characterized by the numerical dominance of Japanese husbands and foreign wives. In 2005, such pairs were 33,116, which is 79.8 percent of all the intercultural marriages. On the other hand, the Japanese wife-foreign husband couples were 8,365, or 20.2 percent.

As for the nationality of women marrying Japanese men, in 2005, China ranked first with 11,644. This was followed by the Philippines (10,242), Korea (6,066), Thailand (1,637), Brazil (311) and others (2,859). And the nationalities of the foreign husbands of Japanese women included Koreans (2,087), Americans (1,551), Chinese (1,015), British (343), Brazilians (261), Filipinos (187), and others (2,738).

Regarding divorces in intercultural marriages, Table 2 reveals that such divorces increase with the increase in intercultural marriages. In 2005, out of 261,917 registered divorces, 15,689 were between Japanese nationals and non-Japanese. Such "international divorces" (*kokusai rikon*) (Matsuo 2005) comprised 5.99 percent of all the divorces in that year. This translates to one out of twenty, similar to the proportion of intercultural marriages. Splits of intercultural marriages have increased, as compared to 12,367 in 2000, and 7,992 in 1995.

Divorces in intercultural marriages are also characterized by the numerical dominance of Japanese husbands and foreign wives, a reflection of statistical dominance of such unions. In 2005, such divorced pairs numbered 12,430, which was 79.2 percent of all the breakups in intercultural marriage. As for the nationality of foreign wives divorced from Japanese husbands, China ranked first with 4,363. This was followed by the Philippines (3,485) and Korea (2,555). The nationality of foreign husbands divorced from Japanese wives included Korean (971), Chinese (492), American (398), Filipino (86) and British (86). Analyzing the trend, Matsuo (2005, 35) anticipates that Japan's "international marriages" and "international divorces" will further increase in number.

Filipino-Japanese Intercultural Marriages: The Roads to the Altar

It has been increasingly difficult for Japanese men to find lifetime partners. In 2005, the average age of women for the first marriage

Table 1: Marriages in Japan by Nationality of Foreign Spouses, 1985-2005

Nationality	1985	1990	1995	2000	2003	2004	2005
Total Number of Marriages	735 850	722 138	791 888	798 138	740 191	720 417	714 165
Both Japanese Partners	723 669	696 512	764 161	761 875	704 152	680 906	672 784
Japanese-Foreign Spouses	12 181	25 626	27 727	36 263	36 039	39 511	41 481
Japanese Husband-Foreign Wife	7 738	20 026	20 787	28 326	27 881	30 907	33 116
Japanese Wife-Foreign Husband	4 443	5 600	6 940	7 937	8 158	8 604	8 365

Japanese Husband-Foreign Wife	7 738	20 026	20 787	28 326	27 881	30 907	33 116
Nationality of Wife							
Korea	3 622	8 940	4 521	6 214	5 318	5 730	6 066
China	1 766	3 614	5 174	9 884	10 242	11 915	11 644
Philippines	...	...	7 188	7 519	7 794	8 397	10 242
Thailand	...	...	1 915	2 137	1 445	1 640	1 637
US	254	260	198	202	156	179	177
England	...	...	82	76	65	64	59
Brazil	...	...	579	357	295	256	311
Peru	...	...	140	145	139	137	121
Others	2 096	7 212	990	1 792	2 427	2 589	2 859

Table 1 *continued*

Japanese Wife-Foreign Husband	4 443	5 600	6 940	7 937	8 158	8 604	8 365
Nationality of Husband							
Korea	2 525	2 721	2 842	2 509	2 235	2 293	2 087
China	380	708	769	878	890	1 104	1 015
Philippines	...	...	52	109	117	120	187
Thailand	...	...	19	67	62	75	60
US	876	1 091	1 303	1 483	1 529	1 500	1 551
England	...	...	213	249	334	339	343
Brazil	...	...	162	279	265	268	261
Peru	...	...	66	124	125	122	123
Others	662	1 080	1 514	2 239	2 601	2 783	2 738

Note: Philippines, Thailand, England, Brazil, and Peru were classified as others until 1991.

Source: Toukei Joho-bu, Heisei 17 Nen Jinkou Doutai (http:/wwwdbtk.mhlw.go.jp/toukei/youran/indexyk_1_2.html accessed on 17 April 2007)

Table 2: Divorces in Japan by Nationality of Foreign Spouses, 1995-2005

Nationality	1995	1999	2000	2001	2002	2003	2004	2005
Total Number of Divorce	199 016	250 529	264 246	285 911	289 836	283 854	270 804	261 917
Both Japanese Partners	191 024	239 479	251 879	272 244	274 584	268 598	255 505	246 228
Japanese-Foreign Spouse	7 992	11 050	12 367	13 667	15 252	15 256	15 299	15 689
Japanese Husband-Foreign Wife	6 153	8 514	9 607	10 676	12 087	12 103	12 071	12 430
Japanese Wife-Foreign Husband	1 839	2 536	2 760	2 991	3 165	3 153	3 228	3 259

Japanese Husband-Foreign Wife	6 153	8 514	9 607	10 676	12 087	12 103	12 071	12 430
Nationality of Wife								
Korea	2 582	2 312	2 555	2 652	2 745	2 653	2 504	2 555
China	1 486	2 476	2 918	3 610	4 629	4 480	4 386	4 363
Philippines	1 456	2 575	2 816	2 963	3 133	3 282	3 395	3 485
Thailand	315	540	612	682	699	678	685	782
US	53	75	68	69	76	75	75	76
England	25	29	41	31	33	17	21	28
Brazil	47	91	92	101	91	101	103	116
Peru	15	25	40	41	45	57	65	59
Others	174	391	465	527	636	760	837	966

Table 2 *continued*

Japanese Wife-Foreign Husband	1 839	2 536	2 760	2 991	3 165	3 153	3 228	3 259
Nationality of Husband								
Korea	939	1 096	1 113	1 184	1 167	1 098	966	971
China	198	320	369	397	447	411	502	492
Philippines	43	59	66	62	77	84	84	86
Thailand	8	20	19	38	36	43	46	30
US	299	356	385	359	364	371	367	398
England	40	42	58	59	58	79	63	86
Brazil	20	39	59	54	78	72	81	81
Peru	7	35	41	52	56	57	56	68
Others	285	569	650	786	882	938	1 063	1 047

Source: Toukei Joho-bu, Heisei 17 Nen Jinkou Doutai (http://wwwdbtk.mhlw.go.jp/toukei/youran/data/5k/1-46.xls, accessed on 17 April 2007.)

was 28.0, a clear rise from 25.2 in 1980 (Tokei Joho-bu 2005). For men, the average age for first marriage was 29.8 in 2005, compared to 27.8 in 1980. Also, in 2000, 42.9 percent of Japanese men aged 30 to 34 were single, while 26.6 percent of Japanese women in the same age bracket were single (Somusho 2000). Percentage-wise, women have more chances than men to get married, but they do not (Jolivet 1997, 146). The tendency to marry late is more pronounced among Japanese women. Feminist perspectives have seemingly impacted on the Japanese women's world-view: They now would rather pursue a professional career and self-fulfillment first before thinking of tying the knot.

Rural Brides (Noson Hanayome)

The shortage of brides was felt especially in rural depopulated areas. Here, unmarried male farmers had difficulty finding lifetime partners because of the perceived low income of farmers, combined with the high possibility that the married couple would live with the parents of the husband. For the same reasons, attempts by a number of local governments in the rural areas to arrange marriages between bachelor farmers and Japanese women have failed. Hence, in 1985, the municipal office of Asahi Town in Yamagata Prefecture, Northern Japan, decided to look for brides from outside Japan. In coordination with a private marriage broker, it mediated the wedding ceremonies of nine Filipino-Japanese couples in the period between August 1985 and September 1986. During that period, the broker escorted nine Japanese men to the municipality of Abucay, Bataan, and introduced them to prospective Filipina brides (Shukutani 1989, 237; Higure 1989, 237). They were soon engaged and the Japanese men left for Japan. A month later the men came back, got married, and brought back their Filipino wives to Japan. The couples began their new life in a rice-growing community in Yamagata. They were welcomed as saviors of a depopulated village as they were expected to bear children and revive the dying community.

The arrival of "rural brides (*noson hanayome*) from the Philippines" caught the attention of other desolate municipal offices all over Japan, which dispatched officials, one after the other, to investigate how to secure brides from the Philippines for their depopulated communities. First among them was the village of Okura in Northern Yamagata. It sought the help of the Japanese Association, Manila, Inc. (Manila Nihon-jin Kai), a nonprofit organization composed of Japanese residents in the Philippines. Many members of the association helped the village find brides in the Philippines. Within a two-month period (August and September 1986), ten Filipino-Japanese couples tied the knot and settled in Okura village (Shukutani 1988). Accompanied by the village mayor and a staff member, five of the Japanese men first went to Bacoor, Cavite, to meet women. After a two-week stay, they had a group church wedding and soon after, the couples left for Japan. The other batch of five men went to Bacoor sometime later (Mori 2002, 83–84).

Furthermore, in 1987, six farmers from a mountain village of Higashi Iya, Tokushima in Shikoku Island, married women from Santiago, Isabela, in Northern Luzon. The marriages were arranged by the municipal office of Higashi Iya, in coordination with a Japanese mediator and the mayor of Santiago. After the matching party in July and the group civil wedding in August, the six couples flew to Japan to commence lives in the deep mountain hamlet of Higashi Iya (Kageyama 1988). Other municipal offices in Yamagata and Akita prefectures in Northern Japan, and in Niigata, Central Japan also arranged marriages with women from the Philippines. These were all coordinated by private marriage brokers who charged exorbitant fees (US$18,000 or more) for their services. The farmers shouldered all the expenses. Some even borrowed money from relatives and commercial money lenders in order to raise the necessary funds.

The marriages emerged as "commercialized" (Nakamura 1994, 17–26), and the media criticized the local governments for being involved in the "purchase" or "human trafficking" of Filipino women (Kageyama 1988; Shukutani 1988). As a result, since the 1990s, local governments in Yamagata have stopped coordinating with marriage brokers, and left the recruiting of Filipino brides to the private brokers (Watanabe 2002, 19). Other local governments followed suit.

The appearance of Philippine brides in Japan coincided with the so-called Philippine mail-order bride phenomenon in Australia. In the 1980s, Filipino women were "ordered" as brides through postal mail by private brokers for Australian men. This became controversial because the activity smacked of human trafficking, as manifested in the cash payment by Australian men who placed orders for brides. Furthermore, cases of serial sponsorship became an issue as a number of Australian men sponsored their fiancées or spouses from the Philippines one after another when they did not like their wives and divorced them. The relationships that resulted from this activity were characterized by a great number of marriage breakdowns, domestic violence, and the failure of some husbands to provide financial support for the women and children (Cunnen and Stubbs 1997, 21; Satake 2000, 186).

In 1990, Philippine President Corazon Aquino signed Republic Act Number 6955, otherwise known as the Anti-Mail Order Bride Law. The official title of the law is "An act to declare unlawful the practice of matching Filipino women to foreign nationals on a mail-order basis, including the advertisement, publication, printing or distribution of brochures, fliers and other propaganda materials in furtherance thereof and providing penalty therefore" (Samonte et al. 1995, 9). With this law, it became difficult for Japanese brokers to arrange meetings between Japanese men and Filipino women in the Philippines. Henceforth, Japanese brokers shifted their major operation to other Asian countries such as China, Korea and Vietnam. At present , Japanese brokers introduce mostly Chinese, Korean, Russian, Vietnamese and Filipino women to Japanese men.

OVERSEAS PERFORMING ARTISTS (OPA)

Since the mid-1980s, a number of Filipino women have come to Japan to work as entertainers either as dancers or singers. Although the Philippine government officially calls them Overseas Performing Artists (OPA), many of them have been forced to work at night as hostesses in clubs and pubs. In 2002, 69,986 (95.5 percent) out of 73,246 entertainers who left for Japan from the Philippines were women. Japan was almost the sole destination of Filipino entertainers, accepting 73,246 (99.4 percent) out of the total of 73,685 (DAWN 2003, 2). Although the guideline of the Japanese Immigration Law bans all the entertainer-visa holders from servicing the customers, i.e., pouring beer or chatting with them, they are forced to do so. Many are also requested to date and accompany the customers to the pubs. Called "dohan," this practice is done to attract customers. Many Japanese men frequent pubs and clubs to look for lifetime partners, not just to relax and unwind from job-related stress. This increases opportunities for both the Filipinas and Japanese men to get acquainted with each other.

In fact, out of sixty Filipino-Japanese couples that the author interviewed or got acquainted with, thirty-six couples first met in pubs and clubs in Japan. Sixty percent of the respondents to the author's questionnaire said their initial rendezvous happened in night spots (Satake 2004, 457; Satake and Da-anoy 2006, 53).

In 2004, out of 134,879 foreigners who entered Japan with entertainer visas, 82,741 were Filipino nationals, comprising 61.3 percent of the total (Table 3). However, in 2005, 99,342 foreigners entered Japan with entertainer visas, a sharp decrease from the previous year. Among all the entrants to Japan with entertainer visas, Filipino nationals numbered 47,765 and constituted 48.1 percent. The decline was caused by the reform of the Japanese immigration policy regarding the entry of entertainers, which, in turn, was a response to the criticism by the US State Department, which said that the entry of entertainers to Japan was turning that country into a breeding ground for human trafficking.

The decrease of Filipino entertainer visa holders, however, did not result in the immediate drop of Filipino-Japanese intercultural marriages. On the contrary, the number of Filipino-Japanese unions,

Table 3: Entry of Entertainer Visa Holders into Japan: 1980-2005

YEAR	ALL NATIONALITY	FILIPINO	PROPORTION OF FILIPINOS TO ALL (%)
1980	20 580	8 505	41.3%
1981	26 615	12 039	45.2%
1982	23 844	9 103	38.2%
1983	25 035	8 375	33.5%
1984	32 952	11 941	36.2%
1985	34 569	17 834	51.6%
1986	44 989	25 996	57.8%
1987	59 693	36 039	60.4%
1988	71 026	41 357	58.2%
1989	60 546	32 636	53.9%
1990	75 091	42 738	56.9%
1991	89 572	56 851	64.5%
1992	84 368	50 976	60.4%
1993	76 242	42 612	55.9%
1994	90 562	53 704	59.3%
1995	59 833	24 022	40.1%
1996	53 952	18 905	35.0%
1997	67 475	31 585	46.8%
1998	73 778	36 550	49.5%
1999	82 305	45 594	55.4%
2000	103 264	60 455	58.5%
2001	117 839	71 678	60.8%
2002	123 322	74 729	60.6%
2003	133 103	80 048	60.1%
2004	134 879	82 741	61.3%
2005	99 342	47 765	48.1%

Note: As for the 2002 figure, Philippine Overseas Employment Administration counts 69,986 as Filipino entertainers who left for Japan as stated in my article.

Source: Ministry of Justice, Shutshu Nyukoku Kanri Tokei Nenpyo (Annual Statistical Reports of Immigration Control); Fujimoto 2006; Revised by the author both those of Filipino wives-Japanese husbands and Filipino husbands-Japanese wives, surged in 2005 (Table 1). The increment might be due to "fake marriages" between Filipino women and Japanese men, which reportedly mushroomed after Japan implemented the immigration control. One source reports that arranged or fixed marriages have become rampant. Accordingly, while Filipina OPAs are still in Japan, they are already paying a large amount of money to their prospective husbands so that they can marry them in the Philippines, and then go back to Japan to work (*Sun Star Manila,* 30 March 2006).

An NHK (Nihon Hoso Kyokai=Japan Broadcasting Corporation) TV program described a different arrangement: Japanese recruiters of entertainers in the Philippines get requests from pub owners in Japan to arrange marriages between Filipino women and Japanese men. The Japanese pub owners who want to procure Filipina OPAs for their *omise* (pubs) ask their customers to "marry" Filipina OPAs. After marriage in the Philippines, the Filipina comes back to Japan with the Japanese "husband," with whom she does not live. She just continues working at the pub. The pub owner pays ¥300,000 monthly to the recruiter in the Philippines. Then the recruiter pays ¥50,000 each to the Filipina as monthly salary and to the Japanese "husband" as monthly reward, keeping the remaining ¥200,000. Hence, if the recruiter arranges ten marriages a year, he earns ¥2 million a month or ¥20 million a year (NHK, 21 August 2006).

Other routes

Other major routes for intercultural encounters include meetings, accidental or otherwise, when Japanese men travel to the Philippines for leisure, business, research, or study. A noticeable pattern is the chain migration/marriage. These are cases in which Filipino women are introduced to Japanese men by a cousin or a sister who is married to a Japanese. In turn, these women start looking for Japanese partners for a niece or a sister. And the chain continues.

THE ORIENTATION OF FILIPINO WOMEN

FAMILY-CENTERED ORIENTATION

Aguilar (1998, 131), in her study on Filipino mothering, points out a Filipino social value that places a premium on social interdependence, or family centeredness, rather than individualism. This is contrasted with the Western practice of mothering in isolated, nuclear, middle-class households, which fosters a feeling of alienation, demobilization, and loss of control by the woman (Aguilar 1998, 131). Furthermore, Tangcangco (1996, 184) claims that Filipino women regard the family as top priority. Hence, Filipino women invariably place a high value on the family or kin no matter where they are. In cases of Filipino women (as well as Filipino men) overseas, this is manifested in regular cash remittances to their families and relatives back in the Philippines. It can be painful and emotionally distressing for Filipino women in intercultural marriages to be denied the opportunity to send money back home (Soriano 1995, 114). This is sometimes the case when Filipinas marry men who grew up in a nuclear family in industrialized countries such as Australia and Japan. The conflict of values can be detrimental to the marriage and may end in divorce. But it can also create wholesome changes in spousal relations.

The strong family-centered value of Filipino women has been observed by their Japanese husbands. Kondo Hajime, a Nagoya cram schoolteacher married to a Filipina, points out that most Filipino women value the "family first principle" (Kondo 2004, 171). Such a mind-set can affect the psyche of Japanese husbands. Miyawaki Makoto, an elementary-school teacher in Takamatsu City, Kagawa, narrates:

> After marriage, my value in life has changed. Now I prioritize my family. Many Japanese prioritize their jobs or they say that it's important to balance job and family. But when I say those things to my Filipino wife, I get scolded. When I go to work on weekends, she asks, "Which is more important, job or family?" As I often tell her that weekend hangouts with

> colleagues are part of the job, she seems to understand what I mean. But she still says that it's no good to do half way, meaning doing something halfheartedly for the family. (Interview, 4 April 2004)

Another Japanese husband once planned to go on a business trip on Christmas day and was strongly opposed by his Catholic Filipino wife. The wife, who could not believe that the husband was going out on that day, said that the family should celebrate Christmas together. He was convinced and postponed his departure until the next day. A Kagawa hotel manager who is wedded to a Filipina from Davao also says that he has also begun to do his share of house chores and child care (Response to a questionnaire, February 2004).

These examples show the life-changing experiences of Filipino-Japanese couples and likewise manifest the conflicting cultural differences as well as areas for negotiating these differences.

The Filipinas' Egalitarian Orientation

The Human Development Report 2006 of the United Nation's Development Program (UNDP) ranks Japan as forty-second and the Philippines as forty-fifth in terms of the gender empowerment measurement (GEM). Accordingly, the GEM value of Japan is 0.557 and that of the Philippines is 0.533. However, in all four indices listed in GEM ranking, the Philippines excels: The proportion of female legislators, senior officials and managers is 58 percent in the Philippines and 10 percent in Japan. The proportion of female professors and technical workers is 61 percent and 46 percent, respectively. The ratio of estimated female- to male-earned income is 0.60 in the Philippines and 0.44 in Japan.

Although the Filipino women who come to Japan do not necessarily hold similar work positions as they do back home, coming from a society where women have a relatively high social position seems to be some kind of sociocultural baggage.

Teresita, one of the six Filipino women married to villagers in Higashi Iya, Tokushima in 1987, but who later moved to Nagoya with the husband, recalls her experience in Higashi Iya.

> One time I was invited for a gathering in the village. So, I dressed up and joined the occasion, which turned out to be a funeral. Only women prepared meals and served men, who just gobbled *sake* (Japanese rice wine) and munched dishes. The male villagers wouldn't even put away the plates. This is incredible in the Philippines. (Interview, 13 July 2005)

Poly, another Filipina who still stays in Higashi Iya , says that she does not like Japan's traditional custom of the husband taking the hot bath first, followed by the in-laws and children. The wife is the last to take a bath (Interview, 23 November 1999).

Daisy, the other Filipina who has remained in Higashi Iya, narrates:

> Women in the Philippines have higher social status. In the male-dominated society of Japan, women have to do almost everything at home and are discriminated against. But since I am a Filipina, I don't comply with Japanese customs that are based on male supremacy and female subjugation. (Interview, 7 June 1997 and 23 November 1998)

Daisy further explains: "A husband might be the pillar of the house (*haligi ng tahanan*), but the wife is the light of the house (*ilaw ng tahanan*). Although a house needs pillars, without lights, the home will be completely dark." Thus she frequently tells her husband that both husband and wife are important in the family. Besides, she has said to her husband from the onset of their marriage, "Once you hit me, I will leave you."

These "empowered voices," which speak of the gender-equality consciousness of Filipinas, are those of the present and erstwhile rural brides who were initially expected to take the place of the traditional Japanese *yome* (brides) in the rural community.

Strength, Everyday Politics and the Psychology of Resistance

Five Japanese husbands share their experiences with their Filipino wives who usually fight to the end when they quarrel. The wives never give in, and engage in an endless battle of words to the point of hurting the pride of their Japanese husbands who were raised in a male-dominated home and society. In the end these men always apologize first, rarely the Filipino wives (FGD, 25 February 2004). Asked about the characteristics of their Filipino wives, many Japanese husbands reply that they are mentally strong, aside from being lively, egalitarian, and talkative. An *udon* noodle manufacturer, Yokoyama Kozo, says that his Filipino wife would not give up what she believes in. And because he is convinced, he surrenders to her like a lamb (Interview, 6 December 2003).

When marital conflicts arise, Filipinas deal with their Japanese husbands in various ways, such as direct confrontation, appeal, or covert strategies. This is everyday politics (Kerkvliet 1991) at home. Covert strategies include the remittance of money to the Philippines from the wife's own secret savings without telling her husband, for some husbands disapprove of giving financial assistance taken from their income. The secret saving, which is called *heso-kuri* in Japanese, is commonly practiced by wives in Japan for emergency family needs and sometimes for personal expenses. Filipino wives resort to *heso-kuri* practice not for such needs but for the needs of the extended family.

From the feminist viewpoint, Estrada-Claudio (1999, 188) contends that it is important to discover the psychology of resistance. Accordingly, the construction of reality within a society is always based on two opposing forces with two opposing goals, namely, the use of force by the ruling class and the resistance of the ruled. She argues that a real challenge to feminists is the search for cultural elements that will serve as the basis for a liberating psychology. In the Filipina-Japanese intercultural marriages, the psychology of resistance among Filipinas is prominent and likewise serves as the basis for a liberating psychology.

Suzuki Nobue (1998, 34), who made studies on Filipina-Japanese couples, also points out that the men's power at home is relative to that of their wives, and the men are in many ways disciplined by their wives to conform to the latter's wishes and ideas.

The positive response of Japanese men to such gender politics is manifested in various ways. One response is a self-imposed decision to go home immediately after work. Another response is to stop smoking, especially after the husband has had major health problems traceable to smoking. In one case, the husband was told by the Filipino wife that she would abandon him unless he stopped the vice (Interview with Okubo Mitsuo, a house clean-up operator, 13 May 2001). Another positive response is the promise of a husband not to go to a local "Philippine pub." Before the marriage he used to frequent pubs, in one of which he met his Filipino wife. And even after the marriage, he could not stop the habit. Upon learning that her husband had gone to the pub, the wife left him, leaving her three-year-old son with him. The husband sought her and was able to locate her. By promising never to go back to the pub, he was able to persuade her to come back to him (Interview with Tabuchi Masaki, a house painter, 25 February 2004).

The Orientation of Japanese Men

Men's liberation

Masuno Kiyoshi cites the image of "men always winning and pushing" as proof of masculinity (*otoko rashisa*) in Japan (Masuno 1985, 130–31). He stereotypes females as passive and waiting to be saved by men. Japanese men with such an orientation tend to oppress Japanese women, especially those who resist domination by them (Satake 1994, 1). Nonetheless, the Filipinas' exercise of power and their attempts to resist male dominance influence their Japanese partners and convince them to be more conscious of equal or negotiable gender relations. Some men stop being domineering.

They try not to impose their will on their wives and instead try to establish a better relationship with them.

A case in point is Tajima Kotaro, who married Jaya in 1997. When Tajima was a college student in Shikoku, he studied for one year at Silliman University in Negros Oriental, Philippines. He is familiar with Philippine culture and speaks some Filipino. Upon graduating from college, he started working at a local government office. There, through the introduction of two Filipina friends married to Japanese, he met Jaya, a Filipina translator in a local timber company. A year later, they were married. This is a typical illustration of the chain marriage discussed earlier. Tajima once declared at a wedding party that "I am now under the hip of my wife (*shiri ni shikarete iru*). But being so is not necessarily bad because it is important to listen to your wife, and not to overpower her." He admits openly that he is a henpecked husband or *under de saya* (under the skirt), to use the Filipino phrase. To borrow the title of a gender study, he refused to be a man (Stolenberg 1990). It can be deduced that he has been influenced by his exposure to Philippine society, where women have a relatively high social position. He often says that Filipino women are strong.

Kondo (2004, 102) also confesses that the biggest change in his married life is that "I am now free from the traditional concept of what is a man (*otoko no kodawari ga naku natta*). I used to behave according to what a man was socially supposed to do." But through the eighteen-year companionship with his Filipino wife, his "masculine pride has been smashed" as she sometimes chides him in front of others, and rebukes him in the presence of their children. "The only pride I have now is that I am free from male-binding value." This is one more example of men's liberation from male chauvinism.

Love and Affection

Some Japanese men do not agree that gender politics explains man-and-wife relations and that negotiations settle conflicts between husband and wife. A Japanese man says, "It's not always the negotiation. I feel hurt if my relation with my wife is just analyzed according to the dynamics of negotiation. I believe that there is an element of love or affection." He illustrates. When his wife asked him if she could leave him for one year for an overseas training required by her office, he agreed out of his affection and respect for her, not out of a negotiated settlement.

Another Japanese husband of a Filipina narrates: "I feel guilty because my wife used to work in a foreign-affiliated company with high salary in Makati. But she gave up her job because I brought her to Japan after the wedding" (FGD, 9 July 2005). He is a scholar from Hiroshima and he met his wife in Manila. There could have been negotiations or even calculations in their decision to settle in Japan, but the fact that he feels "guilty" about it shows that gender politics does not explain it all.

Another case in point is Iwami Hisao, who used to be a full-time electrical engineer at an electric company in Shikoku. After marrying Rachel from Masbate, Philippines, they started their wedded life in Kagawa in Shikoku. Working fulltime at the company, he would leave Rachel alone with her parents-in-law, with whom she had a difficult relationship. To ease Rachel's distress, Iwami decided to resign from his job and engaged in strawberry farming instead. He believed that staying and working together with Rachel in the farm would make her feel better.

Still another case is Imai Ichiro. He used to work in the medical apparatus division of a leading electronics firm in Tokyo. On his business trip to Manila, he met Ester, then an employee at the Manila office of a Japanese trading company. They got married and settled in Tokyo. They have three daughters. The heavy workload required him to leave home at eight in the morning and return home at eight or nine at night. By the time he was ready for dinner, his family would be finished with the meal and he always ate dinner alone. He was like an "alien" from another planet, he recalls. Besides, Ester was working at the cafeteria of a high school in the US Yokota Air Base, a job not compatible with her educational credentials and career experience.

Thus, they decided to migrate to Australia, where Ester's uncle and sister were already residing as migrants. The Imai family moved to Australia in 1999. Both of them were forty-seven years old. Although they were already middle-aged, they made a big life-changing decision all because of Imai's love for his wife.

Imai now works at a medical equipment company while Ester is a data processor in a local government office. Both of them can now properly utilize their educational training and career experience. At present he leaves home with his daughter and wife in the morning, finishes work at five in the afternoon, and comes home with his wife. The family eats dinner together, usually at around 6:30 in the evening. Imai says, "Now I have quality time after 5" (Interview in Sydney on 6 August 1999 and 22 July 2000).

As he abandoned his workaholic lifestyle in Tokyo, it can be concluded that he liberated himself from the stereotypical work-oriented "salary man" who tends to leave all the house chores to his wife. Imai is a showcase of men's liberation. And all of this happened because of his love for Ester.

Cross-Cultural Experiences and Understanding

Contrary to the common view that intercultural marriages are doomed to fail because of cultural differences, this study shows that an intercultural marriage has the potential to enrich both partners' perspectives, depending on each one's world-view, values, and ability to accommodate cultural differences.

Yokoyama Izumi, a staff member of a consumer cooperative, is married to a Filipina from Cagayan de Oro City. They first met in a pub in Takamatsu, Kagawa, where the wife was working as an OPA. They have two children. Although Yokoyama grew up as a Buddhist, he became a Catholic due to the influence of his devout Filipino wife. He is at present a guitarist of the church choir in Sakura Machi, Takamatsu, Kagawa Prefecture, which is composed mainly of Filipino members. He narrates that through association with Filipino friends, he can cross the cultural boundary and experience a world completely different from his business routine. He also recalls that on his son's birthday, their condominium was so crowded with Filipino and other foreign visitors that his son and he had to stay outdoors. He was still grateful that many non-Japanese guests came to the birthday party (Interview, 4 April 2004). Another example is Fukuda Yohei, who married Katherine in 1996. During his college days in Tokyo he traveled to the US, Korea, Indonesia and the Philippines. In the US he felt that Americans looked down on him. But when he visited Asian countries, he did not feel discriminated against and he felt at home. Hence, after coming back to his hometown in Kagawa, where he met Katherine in a local pub, he became attracted to her. When Katherine returned to the Philippines, he followed her and asked her parents for her hand. When he stayed with his in-laws in Manila, he noticed that neighborhood children would come to their house to watch TV, and the in-laws did not seem to mind it at all. He says that this generous attitude toward neighbors, an indication of a beautiful Philippine culture, has long vanished in Japan. He was so fond of the culture of the Philippines and other Asian countries that he opened an ethnic restaurant called "Beer Hoy" (Interviews, March 1997; April 1999; 26 October 2003).

These Japanese husbands accommodate and appreciate cultural differences.

As for Filipino wives, there are a lot of challenges in cross-cultural experiences in a foreign land, such as learning Japanese and dealing with nagging parents-in-laws. And although they would not appreciate nor tolerate male-oriented Japanese values, they observe some aspects of Japanese culture, and as a result, they widen their perspectives through cross-cultural experiences.

A case in point is the acquisition of a driver's license, a rare achievement for many underprivileged Filipino women. A growing number of Filipino wives in Japan pass the actual driving test and the accompanying paper examination in Japanese, an empowering experience in itself. With more mobility and freedom from dependence on their husband for shopping, bringing the children to the daycare centers, and going to church on Sundays, they now relish their independence. Daisy, in a mountain hamlet of Higashi Iya, narrates that the happiest moment of her life in Japan was when she passed the driving test (Interview, 23 November 1998). Most of them would not have driven a car in the Philippines, and their ego has been boosted and their confidence built up.

Also, regarding the "cleanliness" of Japan, Filipino wives observe that the streets are generally free from scattered garbage, unlike in the Philippines. One reason for such a situation in the Philippines, they surmise, can be the lack of enough garbage cans (Satake and Da-anoy 2006, 158), which in turn, can be blamed on inefficient delivery of public services by the local government. They also question the lack of discipline among many Filipinos.

Furthermore, as Filipino wives live longer in Japan, they observe that many elderly people live alone or stay in carehouses separated from their families, which is rare in the Philippines. They also notice that elderly Japanese live on pensions and government health insurance, while their Philippine counterparts rely more on interpersonal relations with their children or relatives for physical, mental, and financial support. Thus, a Filipino wife, Angelita, an English teacher in Nagoya, observes that elderly Japanese people in general appear to be lonelier than *lolo* (grandfather or old men) and *lola* (grandmother or old women) in the Philippines. The sociocultural contrast makes her pity Japanese old people, whom she describes as *kawaiso* (pitiful), and rediscovers a virtue in her homeland (Interview with Angelita, 20 April 2007).

Conclusion

Of course it cannot be denied that there are problematic intercultural marriages. Some of them involve domestic violence and cause marital breakups. This is reflected in the increasing number of Filipino-Japanese divorces. In one instance in Kagawa, under the influence of alcohol, a cram schoolteacher inflicted violent harm on his Filipino wife, who then ran away with her daughter, leaving her son with her husband.

Nevertheless, intercultural marriages cannot be dismissed as altogether problematic. As the findings of the research show, an intercultural marriage provides a venue for cultural diversity and change. This study has argued that an intercultural marriage can enrich as well as broaden the perspectives of its participants, i.e., the Filipino wives and the Japanese husbands. The extent of adjustments and changes depends on the efforts exerted by husband or wife. Intercultural marriages could lead to more gender equality and better relations with deeper cross-cultural understanding.

References

Aguilar, Delia D. 1998. *Toward a Nationalist Feminism.* Quezon City: Giraffe Books.

Cahill, Desmond. 1990. *Intermarriages in International Contexts.* Quezon City: Scalabrini Migration Center.

Cunnen, Chris and Julie Stubbs. 1997. *Gender, "Race" and International Relations, Violence against Filipino Women in Australia.* Institute of Criminology, Monograph Series, No. 9. Sydney: Institute of Criminology, University of Sydney Faculty of Law.

DAWN (Development Action for Women Network). 2003. *Pains & Gains, A Study of Overseas Performing Artists in Japan-from Pre-Departure to Reintegration.* Manila: DAWN.

Fujimoto Nobuki. 2006. *Firipin Jin Josei "Entertainer" No Chokumen Suru Mondai Wo Toshite Nihon No Jinshin-baibai Wo Kensho Suru* [Reflection on Japan's Human Trafficking Issue with Focus on the Problems of Filipina Entertainers]. *Jinken Mondai Kenkyujo Kiyo [Human Right Issue Institute Journal]* 20: 29–63.

Higure Takanori. 1989. *"Mura" to "Ore" no Kokusai Kekkon Gaku* [A Study on Village and My International Marriage]. Tokyo: Joho Kikaku Shuppan.

Jolivet, Muriel. 1997. *Japan: The Childless Society?* New York: Routledge.

Kageyama Shohei. 1988. *Ajia kara kuru Hanayome tachi-Mura no Kokusai Kekkon* [Brides from Asia: International Marriage in the Village]. Hyogo: Nansen Hokuba Sha.

Kondo Hajime. 2005. *Okusama wa Firipina* [My dear wife is Filipina]. Tokyo: Saizu sha.

Masuno Kiyoshi. 1985. *Kazoku* [Family]. Tokyo: Gendai Shokan.

Matsuo Hisako. 2005. *Kokusai Rikon* [International Divorces]. Tokyo: Shuei Sha.

Mori Shigeya. 2002. *Firipin kara Hanayome wo!* [Invite Brides from the Philippines!]. *Bessatsu Tohoku Gaku* [Studies on Northern Japan]. Vol. 4. Yamagata City: Tohoku Bunka Kenkyu Center, Tohoku Geijutsu Koka Daigaku. 74–86.

Nakamura Hisashi. 1994. *Hitobito no Ajia* [Asia of the People]. Tokyo: Iwanami Shoten.

NHK. 2006. "*Jinshin Torihiki Wa Nakuseru Ka?* [Wiping out Human Trafficking?]," *Close Up Gendai,* Tokyo: NHK TV program, 21 August.

Samonte, Elena et al. 1995. *State of the Nation Research Reports, Issues and Concerns of Overseas Filipinos: An Assessment of the Philippine Government's Response.* Quezon City: University of the Philippines Center for Integrative and Development Studies and the University of the Philippines Press.

Satake Masaaki. 1994. *Dansei Kaiho wo Kangaeru* [A Reflection on Men's Liberation]. In *Committee of Beyond Eve and Adam*, ed. Eve to Adam wo Koete: Josei to Jinken wo Kangaeru [Beyond Eve and Adam: Women and Human Rights], 1–9. Kagawa: Shikoku Gakuin University.

_____. 2000. Intermarriage in a Multicultural Society: A Preliminary Research on Filipino-Australian Marriages. *Treatises 102:179–208.* Kagawa: Shikoku Gakuin University.

_____. 2004. Filipina-Japanese Intermarriages: A Pathway to New Gender and Cross-Cultural Relations. *Asian and Pacific Migration Journal* 13 (4): 445–73. Quezon City: Scalabrini Migration Center.

Satake Masaaki and Mary Angeline Da-anoy. 2006. *Firipin Nihon Kokusai Kekkon-Ijuu to Tabunka Kyosei* [Filipina-Japanese Intermarriages: Migration, Settlement, and Multicultural Coexistence]. Tokyo: Mekong Publishing Co.

Shukutani Kyoko. 1988. *Ajia kara Kita Hanayome-Mukaeru gawa no Ronri* [Brides from Asia: Why we invited them]. Tokyo: Akashi Shoten.

Somusho. 2000. *Kokusei Chosa* [National Census]. Tokyo: Somu sho (Ministry of Internal Affairs and Communications).

Soriano, Grace. 1995. "Filipino Families in Australia." In *Families and Cultural Diversity in Australia,* ed. Robyn Hartley. St. Leonard, NSW: Allen & Unwin.

Stolenburg, John. 1990. *Refusing to be a Man: Essays on Sex and Justice.* New York: Meridian.

Sun Star Manila. 2006. "Recruiters: Japan's Migration Law Forcing Entertainers To Go illegal." (http//.www. sunstar.com.ph/static/man/2006/03/30/feat/recruiters.japan.s.migra . . .), accessed on 25 May 2007. 30 March.

Suzuki Nobue. 1998. "Of love and the Marriage Market: Masculinity Politics and Filipina-Japanese Marriages in Japan." Paper presented at the panel, "Men and Masculinities in Contemporary Japan: Beyond the White-Collar Salaryman Model" at the 50th Annual Meeting of Association for Asian Studies, Washington D.C., 26–29 March.

Tancangco, Luzviminda G. 1996. Women and Politics in Contemporary Philippines. Second edition. In *Women's Role in Philippine History: Selected Essays,* ed. University Center for Women's Studies. Quezon City: University of the Philippines Press.

Tokei Joho-bu (Statistical Information Office). 2005. *Heisei 17 Nen Jinko Jotai Tokei* [Population Survey 2005]. Tokyo: Ministry of Labor and Health.

Watanabe Masako. 2002. *Newcomer Gaikoku jin no Zodai to Nihon Shakai no Henyo: Noson Gaikoku Jin Tsuma to Chiiki Shakai no Henyo* [The Increase of Newcomer Foreigners and Change of Japanese Society: Foreign wives in Rural Communities and Change of Local Society]. In *Hen-yo suru Nihon Shakai to Bunka* [Transforming Japanese Society and Culture], ed. Takashi Miyajima and Hirokatsu Kano. Tokyo: Tokyo Daigaku Shuppan-kai.

Interviews

JAPANESE HUSBANDS

Miyawaki Makoto. 4 April 2004.
Yokoyama Kozo. 6 December 2003.
Okubo Mitsuo. 13 May 2001.
Tabuchi Masaki. 25 February 2004.
Yokoyama Izumi. 4 April 2004.
Fukuda Yohei. March 1997; April 1999; 26 October 2003.

FILIPINO WIVES

Teresita. 13 July 2005.
Poly. 23 November 1999.
Daisy. 7 June 1997; 23 November 1998.
Angelita. 20 April 2007.

COUPLES

Imai Ichiro and Ester. 6 August 1999; 22 July 2000.
Frequent meetings with Tajima Kotaro and Jaya between 1997 and 2007
Frequent meetings with Iwami Hisao and Rachel between 1999 and 2006

FOCUS GROUP DISCUSSIONS

With four Japanese husbands. 25 February 2004.
With two Japanese husbands. 9 July 2005.

Chapter 8

A Filipino Husband's Adjustment to Japanese Culture

Efren Ed. C. Flores

I LIVED IN JAPAN FOR A TOTAL OF ABOUT SEVEN YEARS AND HAVE SHARED my life with a Japanese *maybahay* (housewife) for thirty-four years now. I have a lot to share with you, but I will limit myself to my experience as a husband. I will start with the wedding and move on to the story of how Yoko and I managed to stay together through all those years of raising two daughters and a grandson.

The Wedding

Having lived in Japan for about four years before the wedding prepared me to live a life with a Japanese wife. But there were still things that surprised me. I got married in Japan on 18 March 1972, a week after finishing my master's degree at Nagasaki University. The wedding preparations were made weeks ahead. What surprised me most during the preparations was the guest list. Weddings in my home town, Dumaguete City, are characterized by large receptions where entire families and family friends of the bride and the groom are invited. In my hometown, when you invite the head of the family, it is understood that the entire family is invited, starting from the grandfather down to the grandchildren and the in-laws. But for my Japanese wedding, the guest list was very short and precise. The invitations were sent well before the wedding, with an enclosed self-addressed reply postcard. The replies assured us who would come or not. In Japan, when one signifies his intention to attend, he will be present. If it turns out that he/she can not come, he/she sends word before the day of the reception.

Much as I wanted to invite more of my wife's cousins, who also became close to me during my visits to her home town, the guest list for relatives was limited to my wife's father, mother, sister and her husband, uncle and aunts only on her father's side, and two grand-mothers from both sides. It seems that wedding receptions in Japan are only for the older generation. For our friends, Yoko and I were limited to four guests each. It must have been tough for Yoko to select from among her many friends. For me, it was easy. I chose four out of the many fellow Filipino Mombusho (now officially known as Mombukagakusho, this refers to the Japanese government scholarship administered by the Ministry of Education) scholar friends. Since I had only my mother to attend the wedding, I was allowed to invite my university professors in place of my family members.

Fortunately, the wedding ceremony was held at a Roman Catholic Church (celebrated in Japanese, of course), which was bigger than most Shinto shrines. So, even our friends who were not invited to the reception were able to come to the ceremony.

The wedding reception took place without a hitch, as it was held in a downtown hotel where everything was taken care of. There was a hotel staff who guided us through every step of the reception. The food was served in a special lacquered lunch box which the guests could take home after the reception. Special paper bags were provided for the lunch boxes.

At the end of the reception, all the guests were given the *okaishi* (literally, "in return"), which we now call wedding souvenir. In Japan, okaishi is given to say thank you for attending the occasion. Our okaishi was a decorated serving platter which, when put on a stand, can serve as room décor.

SUPPORTING A FAMILY ON A GOVERNMENT SALARY

Back in Manila, the first thing we did was to look for an apartment close to the University of the Philippines (UP), where I was teaching. With the help of my cousins, we were able to get an apartment in UP Village for 300 pesos a month. My take-home pay after all the deductions, was about equal to the house rental! I asked my twin lady cousins to share the apartment with us and also the rent. With what I was making, we could barely make both ends meet. But without my asking, money came regularly from Yoko's parents. I later found out that it was common for parents in Japan to send money to their newly married children to help them out. I did not see this in the Flores family. On the contrary, the opposite was practiced: children, even those who already had their own families, had to send money to their parents whenever they could.

While I was studying in Japan supported by a Mombusho scholarship, I was also receiving my UP salary. I was therefore able to pay for the college education of my younger brother in Manila. When Yoko learned about this, she could not understand why I supported my younger brother's education. To her, that was the responsibility of my parents. I had to explain to her that my older brother also spent money for my college education and it was my turn to do the same for my younger brother. Again, for her, that was still the parent's responsibility, not mine.

Manila is the place where folks from the provinces come to look for a better future. When relatives in the province have financial problems, they usually come to Manila to seek assistance from their relatives. This happened to me a number of times. When it comes to financial matters, I always consult with Yoko. We agreed on a policy that financial assistance to the extended family could only be given after the needs of our own family were met. This meant that I had to earn more in order to help my extended family.

Fellow teachers of my age at UP who were also starting their respective families were not that hard-up because both spouses were employed. Yoko was not working yet. To make both ends meet, I had to look for a part-time job. The decade of the 1970s was the peak of Japanese tourists coming to the Philippines, and tourist guides who could speak Japanese were in demand. This led to the proliferation of private Japanese language schools in Manila. With my command of conversational Japanese, I was hired to teach Japanese in a private language school located in Manila Hotel. The teaching fee then was fifty pesos an hour. I earned an additional income of 600 pesos a month.

Knowing the Japanese wife

I met Yoko when I was learning Japanese at the Osaka University of Foreign Languages. She was a student at the Osaka College of Pharmacy. I knew her then as a typical university student who was influenced by Western culture, e.g., the way she dressed (mini-skirts were the fashion then), the movies we went to, and the music she liked. So, I thought we would be all right in Manila. But to my surprise, she shifted to the "Japanese wife" mode when we got married. She behaved just like her mother at home. I saw this when one day, when I was about to go to work, Yoko was on the stairs, brushing my shoes! I told her at once that I would clean my shoes myself.

Japanese love reading and are trained to read for information. Whenever they need information, they go to the bookstore (and now the Internet). Yoko brought with her a set of cookbooks, a family medicine book, a Japanese-English dictionary and a Philippine guide book, of course all in Japanese. These were the basic books she needed to run our home. This habit of getting information from books, instead of asking friends who might also not know, really helped both of us a lot.

In Japan, the wife buys things needed at home, including appliances. Here in Manila, I had to go with Yoko every time she went shopping, mainly because of the language problem.

Yoko's social life revolved around the Japanese wives of former Mombusho scholars like me. They exchanged notes on their daily lives. When the children were in the elementary grades, Yoko started working at the Japan International Cooperation Agency (JICA) and this expanded her social life, meeting Filipina office mates who were of her age. Before long, she developed a good command of Tagalog, and now behaves more like a Filipina than a Japanese.

The Yamamotos

In Japanese society, the parents of the bride are forever indebted to the groom for taking their daughter as his bride. It is like passing on to the husband the responsibility of taking care of their daughter. So all the men in the household have this responsibility, and thus command great respect and attention at home. This is clearly demonstrated in the order of entering the *ofuro* (Japanese-style bath). The father enters first, followed by the son-in-law. This is in contrast to our Filipino "ladies first" custom. So that I can take the ofuro anytime I please, I give the excuse that the water in the bathtub is still too hot. It really is, anyway!

The other "first in line" treatments are not a problem to me: first to be served at meal time, for example. However, the Yamamotos were surprised when I entered the kitchen to make coffee for myself. Men are not allowed in the kitchen. When one wants anything from the kitchen, he just asks for it and it will be served. I could not adjust to this because making my own coffee was second nature to me. In this respect, they adjusted to me.

I visit Japan at least once a year, either on official trips or on vacation. When in Japan, I always make it a point to visit my in-laws. When I am there I always help in household chores as I do back home. I did not know that my mother in-law felt uneasy with this and finally told me that she felt ashamed that a *gakkobucho* or dean was helping with the household chores. I told her that at home I was "Efren" and not Dean Flores. With that, she felt at ease, and allowed me to help her do the laundry. We got along very well and she always gave me money to buy *pasalubong* (souvenir gifts) for her grandchildren in Manila.

My mother in-law passed away after a long illness. I accompanied Yoko to Japan to pay our last respects. As part of the bereaved family, I did not know what to do and just followed Yoko's every move. My presence was very much appreciated by the Yamamoto family. They thought I would not come because I am not Japanese and not a Buddhist. But I came because I believe that in-laws are part of the family and should be present at family funerals. Filipinos, like Japanese, regard funerals as important as weddings.

Yoko comes from a farming family. The brothers and sisters of Yoko's father were living in the neighborhood, where the *honkei*, household of the eldest son, was the center of the family circle. This is typically shown in the yearly preparation of the yearend *omochi tsuki* or making of rice cakes, which is always done at the honkei compound. The omochi is a must offering, placed at the altar as the New Year approaches. The identification of the eldest son as the center of the clan is not so distinct in the Filipino families.

Back to Japan

As mentioned earlier, support from my in-laws came regularly and this increased with the coming of their grandchildren. Although with my additional earnings I could already support my growing family, I did not refuse the support that came from my in-laws. And I will always be grateful to them for this. This support went on for about seven years, including the years when my entire family was with me in Japan while I was working for my Ph.D. at Hokkaido University on another Mombusho scholarship (1975–1979). During that period, my wife and two daughters were covered by the health insurance of my father in-law. This was possible because my visa status in Japan was "student," making me technically unemployed and therefore with no source of income. Therefore, my wife and daughters were registered as my father in-law's dependents. The Japanese health insurance recognizes dependent relationship of direct descendants as far as the grandchildren.

My Japanese brother in-law, who works with the Japan National Railways, is a model of the Japanese work ethic. He is never late for work. His wife sees to it that he gets to work on time by preparing all the things he needs, like what he should wear and what he should bring to the office. He comes home late as he has to attend to social functions after office hours. And when he reaches home the wife simply asks: "Which would you prefer first, the hot bath or dinner?" She never asks why he is late or whether he has drunk more than enough. She even welcomes him with *gokuro-sama deshita*, which literally means "You have worked hard." Yoko, now very Filipino, still behaves the way a Japanese wife does toward her husband.

The thought of staying in Japan after finishing my Ph.D. came to mind. But there were many locals who had the same training as I did and finding work would not be that easy. Besides, working with an international company would mean staying in metropolitan areas like Tokyo or Osaka, where the standard of living is high. Furthermore, I had a contract with UP to serve the University for two years for every year spent in Japan. And so we returned in 1979.

Manila the Second Time Around

This time, we were better prepared for life in Manila. My finances were good, while Yoko already had enough experience running the house and the kids were going to school. For the children's homework Yoko and I shared the responsibility. I helped the kids with the social sciences while Yoko did the natural sciences and mathematics.

Things got better when Yoko started to work. Now she is like any other Filipino mother who works for a living. She even finds the Philippine situation better than in Japan because here she has two household helpers and a driver, while her sister does not have any of these. When her sister arrives from work she has to prepare dinner. My wife only checks on our cook.

The kids are all grown up now. I retired from government service in 2003 and do my work as an independent consultant at home. This makes my presence at home longer than Yoko, who has two more years to go before retirement.

Chapter 9

The Japanese in the Filipino Cinematic Space

Tito Genova Valiente

THE RELATIONSHIP BETWEEN THE PHILIPPINES AND JAPAN HAS PRODUCED an awareness of cultural identities that are indebted to formal written histories as they are to the nonformal movements of people between the two countries. Japanese persons and personalities have appeared in documents, like paintings and have been portrayed in mass media. Their portrayal is, to a degree, problematic because the feelings between the two countries born out of a long historical relationship have brought out mental files that gravitate between Japanese culture and Filipino culture.

Cultures for the two are spaces that are both metaphorical and temporal, where pictures and perceptions are molded. Sometimes, a feedback mechanism happens when one side, through a protest or acclamation, sends a signal that the perception is accurate or, at least acceptable. In some situations, the images produced are stubbornly held because they fulfill a template against which the particular cultural rendering is satisfying.

A tool like cinema is worth looking into and is much favored by this study because it is both popular and populist. Cinema is a treasure trove of symbols and signs the production of which are influenced by the politics and economics of the land. Dudley Andrew states that "cinema, more than reflecting an era, makes possible such thinking"

(Andrew 1986, 7). For Andrew, cinema can create a way of thinking about something. The images that come out of the Filipino cinema therefore are not from a wellspring of historical and personal linkages, they might as well create images that could push said linkages, bring them to a different level and contouring. Following Andrew, a cinema confirms or alters our way of seeing and "marks a constitutive, not a reflective relation" (ibid., 7). With those dynamics, the Filipino cinema that portrays a Japanese is a site of meanings that contains not a mere interpretation of cultural aspects but a reworking of images and that would inform the way a people would react to those images. This standpoint also presupposes that while the painting of images would be informed by what the perceiver would know about the culture of which that person or artifact is a part, a sense of independent effort is also bestowed on the interpreter.

ARTIFACTS OF DESIRES AND DREAMS

This paper will talk of six films, two of which were made for television. Called "telenovela," the films made for television by GMA-7 are considered significant in their reach and populist appeal. Free TV being the mode of presentation, the works were in a sense assured of a significant audience size.

The first made-for-TV film is given the simple title "Hosto," in Japan the male equivalent of hostesses. The story moves around three men—one gay, one married, and another a drug addict. The value of the story is that, given its small budget, the film is shot in Japan. Whether it was a matter of logistics, the film makes use of Japanese-looking Filipinos. The validation of whether the actors could pass for Japanese rested on the side of the Filipino producers and their casting directors.

The film, on one level, is engaging. Its plot hews to the melodramatic. The social context is eschewed in favor of the personal. This tendency extends to the fact that, while the actors are seen moving around the tourist areas of Asakusa, the surroundings remain a frame for the action. The geography remains a space that could give to the Filipino audience a vision of what Japan looks like—an area of temples and Japanese products.

Outside of the actions that took place before the three migrant workers left the Philippines and which were shot in the Philippines, all the scenes happen in the bar where they work. Since the scenes are filmed in the interior of the bar, there is no way for Tokyo to be portrayed other than in the old Asakusa. The interior shots could have been taken in Manila and it would not have mattered. The Filipinos who were asked to portray the Japanese characters may have come across as credible to the Filipino audience but not to those who know Japan and, at the very least, have heard the Japanese speak in Nihongo.

When the film was shown to an FGD (focus-group-discussion) audience, it was received with incredulity. In one scene in "Hosto" one of the men is caught stealing from an older female client. The client is played by a Filipina who cannot articulate her anger in Nihongo. Confronting the thief, all she can mutter is "dorobo" (thief) and "dame" (bad or that's bad).

"Hosto," as discourse, could not help serving a feast of stereotypes of Japanese culture. In this case, it was the "seppuku," more popularly known among Filipinos as "hara-kiri," the suicide ritual by disembowelment. In this film it is used as a means of telling the story of Filipinos in Japan. The man accused of theft cannot reconcile himself to the fact that his policeman-father does not accept him as his real son. Lonely and separated from his family, he holes himself up in his apartment. Kneeling on the tatami-covered floor, he stages his ritualistic suicide, with the wrong sword, according to one Japanologist who viewed the film.

Why a Filipino would commit suicide in the manner of the Japanese is not clear. What is being said in the scene, however, is that the Filipino becomes a Japanese in Japan and there is no way out of that engagement. If a Filipino is going to regain his honor, he might as well do it in the way that the Japanese would understand. The action should not merely be an equivalent of another act that could reflect a person's honor. The action should contain the character in that culture, and for the Filipino discourse-maker, seppuku is an act he can appropriate. The appropriation is also telling the audience that in this world of migrants in Japan and migrants not generally fitting in the interstices of society, the outsider can find his way back in through the most difficult and the most complex (as it also embodies the inaccessibly religious and culturally intellectual) ritual—the old Japanese way of self-immolation.

The other film is called "Aishiteimasu," not to be confused with a major movie entitled "Aishiteimasu 1941," made in 2004 and directed by Joel Lamangan. The made-for-TV film was directed by another major Filipino director, Peque Gallaga. The film is radical in its attempt to document the life of the Filipino in the presence of the Japanese colonizer. The setting is the Second World War, and the Japanese are already positioned in strategic places in the country. Even as the Filipino guerrillas continue their fight, the Japanese have started creating a semblance of peace and order in the Philippines.

The film takes off from the story of a young Japanese officer who falls in love with a young Filipina. The Japanese officer is presented as good-looking (according to Filipino standards, i.e., the Spanish-mestizo type), intelligent and charismatic. When he talks, he mentions the cultural agenda of the Japanese government more than that of the occupying Japanese Imperial Army.

The audience gets a first glimpse of the young officer astride a horse. The camera is set at a low angle, making the viewer look up to the officer. The viewpoint of dominating/dominated is created from the gaze of the Filipina who, in this scene, has sprained her legs after attempting to run away from the Japanese. Crouching, the Japanese gets into an intimate space with the Filipina, indulging in a tactile relationship with a stranger.

Veering away from the traditional presentation of the Japanese soldier as a figure that evokes fear and detachment, the director has a female companion speak. This woman, who does not view the soldier from the dominated angle, prepares the audience to accept him by describing him as "good-looking" and "kind."

The Japanese soldier then pays his first visit to the home of the Filipina. He meets her mother and proceeds to ask why she is bent on teaching sewing and embroidery to her students. The soldier tells the mother that she should teach them science (this could be interpreted as "technology"). Short of confronting each other, the conversation moves to the language being used. The soldier picks on the English language being used by the mother.

In all these scenes, the dominant image of the soldier is continued. From a visual dominance, a rhetorical and intellectual dominance is put across, a radically different image. In an attempt to capture love in the zone of war, the director communicates the sense that he favors one side, a film opinion that did not yet have the support of the critical mass in the country during the showing of the film. Despite the Filipinos' familiarity with the Japanese during this period, it was still not generally accepted for Japanese characters to be idealized and to be leading men in a film and thus the major carrier of the film's message.

In the film, Gallaga, the director, subverts the desires of people for each other and creates a world where the possible is etched against a background of strong stereotypes. The cultural goods manufactured at the end of the film spool are not politically attractive and may even challenge our memories but they flesh out some small, real stories between the Filipino and that person who was called "the enemy" at that point in Philippine history.

These cultural images, while constituting what the artist could exhume from extant narratives, also reflect the social history of the period that produced the film. By the 1980s the Japan-bound Filipinos could be described as "acquainted" with the daily depiction of Japanese culture. Kinship has been formed out of intermarriages, and relationships have been forged between Japanese employers and Filipino employees. The dominant/dominated relationship structure is still there but it is carried onto the level that is market-driven. The

Filipino and the Japanese are, in a sense, operating in the interstices of their cultures where the nonformal takes the place of the formal. In that realm, historical documents about abuse and domination are supplanted by the new phenomena of countries with peaceful and friendly relations.

Cinema thus creates a bigger space that can accommodate the Japanese still as a soldier, still the enemy, but already loaded with the qualities of potential lover or partner. In another historical dimension, one can talk about this depiction as a crime. In the realm of the imagination, the present historical realities are presaged in favor of the individual, the personal, the noncollective.

The idea of the Japanese man as the would-be partner of the Filipino woman is not original to "Aishiteimasu." This brave premise is developed early in the film space of "Tatlong Taong Walang Diyos" (Three Godless Years). The title refers to the three years of Japanese occupation and comments on the general impression of the Filipinos about the absence of religion (meaning, absence of mercy) in the Japanese social fabric vis-à-vis the surplus of religiosity in Filipino society, although the excess may be nominal.

The film centers around the usual love triangle, but this time made insidiously complex because the woman has to choose between the first lover, a guerrilla who disappears into the mountains to fight the Japanese, and a young Japanese soldier who is willing to protect and love the Filipina in wartime. The Japanese soldier also happens to be half-Filipino, a lineage that softens the accommodation that this film offers in the mid-1970s, some thirty years detached from the end of the real Asia-Pacific War.

In the language of cinema and popular culture, the message of the film "Tatlong Taong Walang Diyos" is allowed in the solitude of the viewing and helps the audience with what Andre Bazin calls the "refusal of social responsibility" (1968, 99–102). The burden of facing the dilemma that the characters enact before the Filipino audience is diminished and made lighter and bearable because the film is major and the actors are popular and the leading lady is phenomenal. The debate that ensues does not create violence but only a bracketing of a story so that what it purports to say is tolerable, acceptable, and palatable.

SUBVERTING INTERPRETATIONS

In 2002, at the height of the claims for restitution and justice from the old women who claimed they had been "comfort women," a euphemism for women who were conscripted to serve the sexual needs of the Japanese soldiers from the warfront, a film was released on what is still considered a rare and unvalidated phenomenon of "comfort gay." The questioning of the phenomenon is technical: it has already been deduced and admitted that there were homosexual relations during the war and that there were soldiers who solicited sexual services from men.

The film was "Markova: Comfort Gay," a movie based on the life of Walter Dempster, a gay man living in the home for the aged gays somewhere in the Philippines. Except for the confession of the old man who decided to present another side of the comfort women phenomenon, the film's source materials have not been supported by any historical validation.

As a medium that is also constitutive, the cinema that is based on a monological confession is important for what it really wants to put across. In "Markova" we find a document that forms an image of the Japanese soldier and his sexuality and violence placed in the context of an aberrant or deviant or alternative gender relations. That the Japanese has in him the possibilities of a lover shows that the Japanese, for the first time in a formal filmic documentation, can also be gay.

In a society where the gay identity is still a crucial issue insofar as acceptance and tolerance are concerned, the identification of the soldier whose cultural umbilicus is seen as attached to that locus of Oriental machismo, the samurai is both a daunting and an ideological incursion into another space for the Japanese in the Philippines. Markova may not be a good film but its formation of an alternative space in which to situate the Japanese man prepares the reader/viewer for another portrayal of the Japanese.

LOVE IN WAR

The Japanese in a marginalized gender position receives artful if not ponderous reflection in "Aishiteimasu 1942." Given the peripheral imaging of the homosexual or gay in the mainstream heterosexual culture, the film eventually takes on a complex web of perspectives. In this complex retelling, the Japanese soldier is depicted as the lover of a woman who happens to be a man in a woman's dress. Even at the end of the movie, the soldier is not painted as gay.

The film's title may be about gay relationships in times of war and may come across as a work that faces head-on the issues of alternative relationships, but this is at best deceptive. The film remains a conventional appraisal of "gayness." The Filipino may have been gay from the very start but his crossdressing is a function of a patriotic duty. By being a woman, "a pretty woman" in the eyes of the Japanese, the Filipino assumes a gender role that will be used by the guerrillas for spying. Once more, in the tradition of war films in the Philippines, the female spy who is demonized by the society is vindicated by the position that his death reclaims for him. In fact, the whole town debates after so many years the contribution of a gay man to the fight for freedom, a sphere where influence is male-dominated and straight.

Despite the traditionalism it rides on, the film offers an opportunity for the Filipino to negotiate his understanding or perplexity regarding the Japanese as a human being, and especially the Japanese warrior or man. This opportunity lies in the realization by the woman/man that his/her Japanese lover knew all the while that she was a he. This is a realization that was shared by two members of the audience during one of the screenings of the film. One said: "Ay bakla pala ang Hapon!' (Oh the Japanese is gay!). The other remarked: "Ah, may bakla palang Hapon?" (There are gays among the Japanese?). In those question marks and exclamation points are both socially validated bigotry and points of ignorance from which all forms of cultural mental filing can take place. That the Filipinos, as audience, can be ignorant and, to a degree, capable of bigotry or racism, is indicated by those comments.

VIEWS FROM THE OFF-CENTER

A more critically acclaimed film, "Panaghoy Sa Suba" (translated as "Call of the River") problematizes the space for the Japanese in the Philippine life. Once more the period is the Second World War. A small town is occupied by a band of Japanese soldiers who are, it seems, detached from the major occupation force. At the center of the narrative is a river, pristine, quiet, eternal. The town, in the hinterlands of Bohol, stands as a figurative town representing a Filipino territory that is threatened but not totally ruled by the Japanese.

Before the coming of the Japanese, the town has an industry run by an "ugly" American. In a counterspace given by the film, the American stereotypically propped up as gentle and benign has his role subverted. He is the town villain, the contravida. He is attracted to a woman who later also attracts the attention of the Japanese officer.

The American is uncouth and racist, while the Japanese soldier in this film is pictured as a thinker, one who weighs things thoroughly, a figure with a moral compass, in a medium that has trivialized them as characters for the last fifty years. The other films mentioned may have gradually created the rational psychology of the Japanese person, but "Panaghoy" pushes the ante further and proceeds to mount the clear-headedness of a Japanese versus the muddled morals of the American. In the end, we have the cinema that attempts to tell the story of the war from the periphery with characters depicted away from the mainstream. In this marginal village, the marginal characters in the national tale of occupation and violence are at the center of the events. Suffice it to say also that the film is in Cebuano, in a language that annihilates the filter of the central language that is Pilipino and Tagalog. The film thus is both a source of cinematic and linguistic spaces, where discourses about societies and the notions of person are explored.

In these cinemas, the concepts explored are dynamic entities, the appropriation of which is dependent, to a great degree, on the perceivers. This idea would make the viewer realize that "the person is not something one can study and provide for; he is something one struggles for" (Percy 1999, 576).

No Problem of Interpretation

There is no problem in interpreting what is Japanese. As the theoretical underpinnings of this paper put across, culture is conjunctural and not essential. There is really no essence that can be imbued in culture. Cultures move and in this globalized age, they are transferred, copied, transplanted, officially constructed in another site and validated in the site that is deemed original.

If one is a purist, then James Clifford would call this the process of "pure products going crazy" (1988, 1–17). Here, in this global age, the search for authenticity is a difficult enterprise. James Clifford may have been describing the Japanese being described by the Filipinos and the Filipinos trying to come to terms with their imagination and valorization of their images about the Japanese when he said "Intervening in an interconnected world, one is always, to varying degrees, 'inauthentic': caught between cultures, implicated in others" (Clifford 1988, 1).

The Filipinos are caught in their textbook knowledge about Japan that has been built around stereotypes. While they describe Japan, the Filipinos are implicated in their own cultures that connect them to the European, by way of Spain, and the Americas, through the Americans. It cannot be avoided that they would be in awe of the Oriental. Their avowed Spanish heritage is not questioned and their American "upbringing," together with the Spanish, creates the Orientalist in the Orientalist backyard.

Mixed and putatively Westernized, the Filipinos need to look for that Other, that group of people vastly different from them. This attitude marks the Filipino viewer taking in anything Japanese as not only unique but also pure. The reverse happens for the Filipinos. In the Filipino mind, the Philippines is somewhere in between, also strong and also unique because it combines the West and the East. Japan is purely East, where aesthetics are so different and incomprehensible they might as well use the native terms for what Japan marks as beautiful.

In the Japan of the Filipinos lies the seed of what Darrell William Davis called the "interrogation of history" (Davis 1996, 12). Histories are questioned by films. Where the auteur goes to a great extent of researching for authenticity, there is in that artistic space of cinema a possibility for a discourse that comments on what happened. As in the selectivity of details and events, the artist is free to make his rendition of history and the characters in those histories.

References

Andrew, Dudley. 1986. "Film and Society: Public Rituals and Private Space." *East-West Film Journal*, I, 1 (December): 7–22.

Clifford, James. 1988. *The Predicament of Culture, Twentieth-Century Ethnography, Literature, and Art.* Cambridge, Massachusetts: Harvard University Press.

Davis, Darrell William. 1996.. *Picturing Japaneseness. Monumental Style, National Identity, Japanese Film*. New York: Columbia University Press.

Percy, Walker. 1999. "The Loss of the Creature." In *Ways of Reading: An Anthology for Writers,* ed. David Bartholomae and Anthony Petrosky, 565–80. Boston: Bedford St. Martin's.

Chapter 10

Gatas: Sa Dibdib ng Kaaway (In the Bosom of the Enemy)

Ronaldo L. Santos, Jr.

Our history and culture are tremendous sources of inspiration and imagination. Filipino and Japanese interaction during the Japanese occupation (1941–1945) presents a clash of cultures through the hands of destiny. The sad experience of war is revisited by director Gil Portes in his 2001 movie, *Gatas: Sa Dibdib ng Kaaway.*

The film is a riveting account of the story of Pilar, a local fisherman's wife who agrees to be wet nurse to a Japanese captain's newborn son in exchange for her husband's freedom.[1] Set during the Second World War, it is a period film that aims to showcase a different facet of war history. Far from the usual themes of blood and gore of fighting, pride, nationalism, and the flag, the film illustrates not the violence of war but the emotions and passions that spring from the depths of human nature.

Set in the simple, beautiful scenery of rural Philippines of the 1940s, the film starts with the arrest of Diego, Pilar's husband, by Japanese soldiers. Accused of being a member of the guerrilla movement, Diego is incarcerated and tortured. Upon hearing the unfortunate news, Pilar hurries to the Japanese camp and pleads for the release of her husband. The captain, Hiroshi, is kind and just and has a newborn son, Tetsuya. His Filipina wife died in giving birth to Tetsuya. Hiroshi is completely different from Kojima, the ruthless other Japanese officer who mercilessly kills Filipinos.

After some time, Diego is released in exchange for Pilar agreeing to feed Tetsuya from her breasts because the supply of powdered milk has run out. By nursing the son of a Japanese captain, Pilar earns the enmity of the townsfolk and is isolated from the society. Tension is created between her and Diego. Still full of hatred of the Japanese who tortured him during incarceration and wanting to take revenge, Diego eventually joins the guerrilla movement.

While Hiroshi is away for a mission for three days, Diego's companions ask Pilar to kidnap Tetsuya so that they can make him a hostage in exchange for a captured Filipino guerrilla. If she does not agree, her own daughter, Luningning, will be kept away from her. Pilar reluctantly agrees, but later changes her mind. Maternal instinct and pureness of heart overpowers her. In the eyes of her countrymen, however, what she did is "betrayal." When she comes home, her husband and child are gone, and her house is burned to the ground. No one in the neighborhood offers a helping hand because they are afraid of the guerrillas.

Left alone, she eventually warms up to Hiroshi, who has provided her comfort and friendship. They become lovers. Meanwhile, Diego himself enters into sexual relations with Soledad. One day, Diego and Pilar meet, but Diego refuses to let her see their daughter.

Once again, the guerrillas ask for Pilar's cooperation for the sake of their cause. This time, she is asked to poison Hiroshi and the other Japanese soldiers. Pilar agrees, reluctantly, but once again, changes her mind.

Liberation ends the war, and the Americans rescue the Filipinos. Their arrival emboldens the guerrillas to attack the Japanese camp. At the end of the bloody struggle, the film ends showing Pilar carrying baby Tetsuya in her arms, running towards the office of Hiroshi, only to find him dead. He has committed seppuku. She also sees her husband Diego, drenched in blood. He has been killed in an encounter with the other Japanese soldiers. Pilar never sees her daughter again. She leaves the town with Tetsuya, unforgiven by her neighbors.

Who is the Enemy?

From the title alone, with the word "enemy," it appears that the movie somehow questions the meaning of the word "enemy" and subverts it. Quite contrary to what is inscribed in our history books, the film is a cornucopia of notions that oppose our perception of who really are our enemies and friends. The tale of Pilar proposes a vision of society that blurs the borders of conventions and asks us to look beyond the obvious and deep into the person's humanity.

The film tells us that not all Japanese are blood-lusting samurai. Our image of the Japanese soldier, formed out of numerous accounts of massacres during the Second World War, is that of a ruthless, callous, brutal, cold-blooded person. There may be some truth to this, and the tales of those left behind who experienced such tragedies attest to it; but it would be wrong to generalize.

The following lines uttered by Hiroshi tell us about how war shapes the minds and actions of persons: "Pilar, gusto kong malaman mo . . . kaming Hapones, mga kaibigan. Pero sa giyera, dahil sa giyera, maraming tao, kahit kaibigan, kahit Hapones, kahit Pilipino, nagiging hayop . . . ikaw, ako. Sana hindi tayo gano'n."[2] (Pilar, I want you to know that the Japanese are your friends. But in war, because of war, many people . . . friends, Japanese, Filipinos become animals . . . you, I. I wish it were different.)

Thus, the question of whether someone is a friend or a foe should be answered in the proper context; in this case, in the context of war. And because war is, in the words of Hiroshi, something that turns humans into animals, would it be correct to expect rationality in times when ideological and nationalistic positions numb and structure the minds and hearts of people? Who is Pilar's enemy: the just, kind, and comforting Hiroshi, or her inconsiderate, vengeful, unsympathetic husband Diego? Who is her friend: her husband who raped her because of wrong suspicions, or Hiroshi, the caressing, passionate Japanese lover? Which is more human: to take Tetsuya as hostage and risk the life of the helpless child, or to risk being condemned by her neighbors as traitor for doing what she thinks any mother would do for a child, regardless of whether it is Filipino or Japanese?

Hiroshi is a rare breed of Japanese, and yet he is at once a product of the Japanese culture, at least, in the eyes of the movie maker:

Hiroshi:	Wala akong hinihintay dito kundi ang wakas. (I await nothing here but Death.)
Pilar:	Bakit 'di ka pa tumakas, kung gano'n? Anong uri kayong lahi gayon na lang pumatay at magpakamatay? (Why don't you escape? What kind of a people are you, who are just willing to die and kill?)
Hiroshi:	Saan ako tatakas? Hahabulin ako ng kahihiyan sa kabilang buhay.[3] (Escape is impossible. Shame will haunt me even in death.)

The Japanese soldier is portrayed here as one whose acts are rooted in his intense pride and love of country. He kills not because he hates the Filipinos, not because he is naturally bloodthirsty, but because it is expected of a Japanese soldier.

Those Left Behind

From a different angle, the film also introduces the plight of the Tetsuyas, persons born out of a Japanese and Filipino union. In one of the first scenes, before she gives birth to their child, Hiroshi talks to his wife Carmen:

Hiroshi:	. . . ama ng ano? Babae o lalaki? (I'll be a father of. . . ? Girl or boy?)
Carmen:	Maski ano. (It doesn't matter.)
Hiroshi:	Hapones or Pilipino? (Japanese or Filipino?)
Carmen:	Ikaw . . . ano sa palagay mo? (What do you think?)
Hiroshi:	Pareho . . . bakit hindi pareho? (Both . . . why not?) Ikaw, ako, siya . . . anak ko . . . ang anak natin . . .

> Siya ang bagong Hapones . . . bagong Pilipino[4]
> (You, I, the child . . . my child . . . our child . . .
> It is the new Japanese . . . the new Filipino.)

Upon the death of Carmen, Hiroshi muses: "Hindi kailanman naintindihan ng iyong mga kalahi at ng aking mga kadugo ang pag-ibig natin . . . pero para sa akin, ito'y isang pagbubuklod na sagot sa nagaganap na digmaan, kaya ito'y may katuturan . . .[5] (Your people and my people never understood our love for each other. But for me, it is a bond that answers questions about the current war. That's why, it has a wider meaning.)

Sadly, what Hiroshi wishes as the country's future has been actually considered as shameful products of war and history. Filipino wives of Japanese, together with their children, who were left behind "tried to hide their racial origin for fear of Filipino reprisals, and out of shame for the defeat of Japan in the war" (Jose 1998, 338). Pilar and Tetsuya leave their town, and remain unforgiven by the townspeople. "It was only in the 1980s that many of them began to come out in the open. Some expressed a desire to see Japan, and many fulfilled the wish; still others expressed a desire to be recognized as Japanese citizens. The paper work to prove their Japanese ancestry is laborious, and only a few have succeeded in getting Japanese citizenship" (ibid.).

Notes

1. The role of the Japanese captain was played by a Filipino whose screen name for this movie was Kenji Motoki. He is Kenji Marquez in real life. He happens to look Japanese. He is the great grandson of Jose P. Laurel, president of the Philippine republic under the Japanese Occupation (notes supplied by Tito Valiente, film critic).

2. All direct quotes and passages are taken from the film, VCD version, exclusively distributed by Regal Homes Entertainment., Regal Homes Video. Film Released January 2001. This particular quote is taken from the scene wherein Pilar is in Hiroshi's office, pleading for the release of her husband, Diego (disc 1).

3. These lines are taken from the conversation between Pilar and Hiroshi by the seashore, before the coming of the American soldiers (disc 2).

4. Disc 1.

5. Disc 1.

References

Gatas: Sa Dibdib ng Kaaway. 2001. VCD version. Regal Home Entertainment. Regal Home Video.

Jose, Lydia N. Yu. 1998. "Philippines-Japan Relations: The Revolutionary Years and a Century Hence." In *Philippine External Relations: A Centennial Vista*, ed. Baviera, Aileen San Pedro, and Lydia N. Yu Jose. Manila: Foreign Service Institute.

Chapter 11

The Role of Japanese NGOs in Philippines-Japan Relations

Junefe Gilig Payot

This chapter aims to determine the impact of Japanese NGOs (JNGOs) on Philippines-Japan relations. JNGOs are agents of people-to-people relationships: Japanese JNGO staff members interact with Filipino JNGO staff members, with the communities, and with local partner NGO staff members. Impact refers to images and impressions created in the Japanese and the Filipinos as they interact while engaged in the projects and activities of JNGOs.

Most studies on bilateral relations tend to dwell on official relationships and to focus on government-to-government diplomacy. But before there were governmental relations, there were only people-to-people relations. In the case of Japan and the Philippines, Japanese fishermen and traders, mostly from Nagasaki, would sail to Manila in October and May and sail back to Japan in June or July. They even formed small communities (*Nihon machi)* in Manila, Cagayan and Pangasinan (Jose 1998, 279). Even when governments came into the picture, people-to-people relations remained very important in shaping the bilateral relations.[1]

Any personal dialogue between people from different countries is inevitably also a dialogue between cultures for "human beings are both objects and conveyors of cultural influences" (Jose 2005, 40).

Thus, people-to-people relations can be seen in the context of cultural interaction between the Philippines and Japan.

The spheres in which cultural relations between the Philippines and Japan take place may be classified into (1) Japan's international cultural policy, (2) cultural exchanges provided by private organizations that have taken upon themselves this task, and (3) cultural exchanges or exposure naturally resulting from bilateral national contact, even without deliberate efforts (Jose 1998, 327). The JNGOs in the Philippines belong to the third sphere. Cultural exchange is not their primary activity but the inevitable personal relations between the Japanese JNGO staff, their Filipino local partners and the Filipino community where they work result in some sort of cultural exchange.

In the first sphere, cultural relations are one-sided because of the unequal economic development of Japan and the Philippines, although in the 1990s Japan began to include in its cultural program the introduction of Philippine arts and culture to Japan. (Jose 1998, 327). In the second sphere, it is not one-sided but still unequal because there are more organizations in Japan than in the Philippines that can allocate resources for cultural activities. In the third sphere, it is "less unequal, although still a little bit tilted in favor of Japan. There is more evidence of Japanese influence in the present Philippine society than there is of Philippine culture in Japan. It seems that it takes less time for many Filipinos to appreciate Japanese culture, than it does for most Japanese to appreciate Filipino culture" (ibid.). This chapter wants to explore whether in their interactions, Japanese and Filipinos are more or less equally influenced by each other, or whether one of them tends to have more influence than the other.

Corollary to this, the chapter wants to know the impact of JNGOs on Philippines-Japan relations by looking at impressions and images the Japanese and Filipinos who interact within the JNGO projects have of each other. For most Filipinos, historically, Japan has been curio, inspiration, enemy, and model (Jose 2000). Japan was an inspiration to many Filipinos who were longing for independence in the 1920s and 1930s. Japan as enemy refers to the Second World War and the Japanese occupation of the Philippines, an image that today still affects the views of Filipino intellectuals (ibid., 8). In the 1960s Japan was considered a model of economic development. At present, many Filipinos still view Japan as a model, given its economic dominance in Asia. But this view is tempered by the knowledge that Japan and the Japanese have traits that are not likeable to Filipinos. This sort of knowledge is gained through more intimate person-to-person relations such as those between Filipino students and their Japanese classmates, their experience in Japanese dormitories; relations of overseas Filipino workers with their Japanese employers, the neighborhood, and so on. In the case of the Filipino communities where JNGOs operate, what mutual impressions have been created?

Two JNGOs are chosen as case studies, selected because of their relatively long experience in the Philippines and their involvement in long-term projects. A preliminary survey done by the author showed that most Japanese NGOs in the Philippines were founded between the late 1980s and mid-1990s. The two JNGOs used in this study were founded during that time and therefore represent most of the JNGOs in the country in terms of length of experience.

These JNGOs are the Intercommunication Center for Asia and Nippon (ICAN) and the Health Assistance and Neighborhood Development Support Incorporated (HANDS). ICAN was founded in 1995 while HANDS was founded in 1996. The former is involved in urban development work while the other one is in rural development, both long-term activities. They both have been recipients of Japanese government funds, attesting to the high valuation given to them by the Japanese government. ICAN directly works with the community, while HANDS partners with local NGOs. Moreover, ICAN members are younger than the members of HANDS. The average age of HANDS members is about sixty years.

Thus, while the similarities between ICAN and HANDS (long presence in the Philippines and engagement in longterm projects) formed the basis for selecting them as case studies, serendipity adds the differences as an interesting basis for contrast which may affect their respective impact on Philippines-Japan relations: one is urban, the other is rural; one is directly involved in the community, while the other is involved only indirectly; HANDS members are senior citizens, being mostly in the sixties or above, while most ICAN members are relatively young, being in their forties or fifties.

HISTORY OF JNGOs IN THE PHILIPPINES

According to a study of the Asian Community Center 21 (ACC21), there are 86,000 citizen-based organizations in Japan, 400 to 500 of which are involved in international development assistance (ACC21 2006). Of these 400 to 500, eighty to ninety have been involved in the Philippines, making the Philippines "the most popular country for Japanese NGOs" (ACC21 2006).[2]

According to the study, the Philippines is the most popular destination mainly because of its geographical proximity to Japan (Philippines-Japan NGO Symposium 2006).[3] It must be remembered that geographical proximity was also a reason why contact between Japan and the Philippines "began early and as naturally as the flow of the sea and the direction of the wind would have it" (Jose 1998, 279) and why the Philippines would go on to host the largest number of Japanese in Southeast Asia in the decades before the Second World War (ibid., 292).[4]

By most accounts, the Organization for Industrial, Spiritual and Cultural Advancement (OISCA), which started in October 1961, was the first JNGO in the Philippines. Japanese Rotary Clubs began projects in the Philippines in the early 1970s. The Ajia Idobata-kai (Deep Well Society of Asia) started to teach the traditional Japanese method of digging a well to a group of farmers in Mindanao in the 1980s. The Asia Community Trust (ACT) and the Japan Fund for Global Environment (JFGE) are some of the active organizations primarily in environmental protection projects (Jose 1998, 326). The head office of OISCA in the Philippines was opened in December 1973 (OISCA 2002, 36–39). One of its earliest projects in the Philippines was the

OISCA Technical Training Alumni Association Center (OISCA-OTTAA) Canlaon Training Center in Negros Oriental which was opened in 1979.[5]

One of the significant developments in the history of Japanese NGOs in the Philippines was the recent formation of the Philippines-Japan NGO Partnership (PJP), a loose network of Philippine and Japanese NGOs formed in January 2006. It is a significant development because before this there was no network or forum where several Philippine and Japanese NGOs could interact. There were only isolated partnerships between individual Japanese NGOs and their partner Philippine NGOs or communities. Before this, even the JNGOs themselves did not interact with each other.

A parallel grouping called the Japan-Philippine Network (JPN) was also formed among NGOs in Japan. The group helps in the advocacy by making Japanese ODA more NGO-friendly and in particular to help push for the Philippine NGO-envisioned funding mechanism by the Japanese government.

THE INTERCOMMUNICATION CENTER FOR ASIA AND NIPPON (ICAN)

ICAN started in General Santos City as the "personal commitment" of a Japanese individual who in 1994 started giving scholarships to children in General Santos City in partnership with a local NGO. Its commitment in Payatas, which is the focus of this study, started in 1999 with Ito Yoko, who in that year came to Payatas to donate used boots from Japan to the scavengers. Payatas is a very poor and dirty community. Phase Two sections of this twenty two-hectare area where ICAN operates is the disposal site, which became notorious worldwide because of the so-called "trash slide" on 10 July 2000 (*Japan Times,* 5 November 2002) which killed hundreds of families who lived at the foot of the mountain of garbage. The lives of hundreds of scavenger families revolve around this dumpsite. Thus, it can be said that ICAN is right at the geographic and socioeconomic center of Payatas.

The office of ICAN in Manila has a staff of seven—four of them Japanese and three Filipinos. ICAN hired the Filipino staff to assist the Japanese staff in their operations because of the Filipinos' advantage as "insiders" who can speak fluent Tagalog and who know the local culture very well. Although all the Japanese staff except the nurse are articulate in Tagalog, there are still some nuances they do not understand, and this causes problems.

Realizing the danger of working in the dumpsite after the trash slide, ICAN members decided that they had to do something to give the families an alternative source of livelihood. According to Ito, "The best way to free the people of Payatas from such an existence is to provide better education and vocational training, to give them a chance to find other jobs . . ." (*Japan Times,* 5 November 2002).

So they gave them vocational training. The group of mothers who joined the training is known as the *Sikap Pangkabuhayan ng mga Nanay sa Payatas* (SPNP) and is now ICAN's partner in its programs.

ICAN sells its products made by the Filipino mothers in trade fairs in the Philippines and Japan. They have to be strict with the quality of the products that the mothers make because Japanese customers demand high quality.

THE MOTHERS SPEAK: ASSESSMENT OF PROJECTS

The paper will show in this section how the mothers assess the projects of ICAN. Three mothers were interviewed individually about their views on the medical, feeding, and livelihood programs.

Medical Program. ICAN provides medical checkups twice a week and affordable medicine which the mothers unanimously say is a big help to them and their children. ICAN is also involved in the Directly Observed Therapy Short Course (DOTS) that currently has twenty-eight persons with tuberculosis (TB) enrolled. In this program DOTS, with the help of the barangay, looks for people with symptoms of TB.

Feeding Program. There are now two groups of children in the feeding program, which used to cater only to malnourished children. But ICAN has now prioritized those who are in their DOTS program. At present there are twenty children with tuberculosis who are enrolled in the program and ten who are malnourished. According to the mothers, the feeding program is very important for mothers who really cannot feed their children.

Livelihood. ICAN supports two livelihood programs for mothers in Payatas. It has three main products—handicrafts, crocheted items, and teddy bears—which are sold by ICAN in the Philippines and Japan. All three mothers say that the income they get from the livelihood program of ICAN is substantial. According to one mother, the weekly average of 1,000 pesos she earns from this livelihood program substantially adds to her husband's meager income and is enough for the school allowance and transportation expenses of her six children.

The other livelihood program is for mothers who make *bayong* (native shopping bag). The eleven mothers in this livelihood program are also the mothers of the children in the feeding program. The program was started for the mothers who were unable to bring their children to the feeding program because they had to scavenge. Now they make bayong in the venue of the feeding program instead of going out to scavenge.

In bayong-making, the mothers earn as much as 300 pesos per week, a substantial amount that is more than what the mothers can get from scavenging. Also, the fact that they no longer have to scavenge means that they no longer expose their children, especially breast-feeding babies, to unsanitary conditions as much as before.

Aside from the economic benefits, the mothers also say that they appreciate the livelihood program because it allows them to be near their families most of the time since it is community-based, and also allows them to enjoy the company of other mothers. Moreover, being earning women makes them feel good and makes them realize that they, too, can work, not just their husbands.

Thus, it is clear from the foregoing that the mothers generally assess the ICAN projects positively. This is especially true of the livelihood program, which is understandable, given the economic poverty in the area.

MOTHERS' PERCEPTIONS OF THE JAPANESE STAFF

In this section, the paper will show the mothers' attitude toward the Japanese staff of ICAN. There is much opportunity for interaction between the mothers in the community and the Japanese staff because the Japanese members of ICAN go to the community regularly. In all these interactions, impressions and generalizations are created. But even as they generalize on the basis of their experience, they also individualize. In these interactions, the Filipino mothers find Japanese characteristics they like and do not like, as well as characteristics they would like to emulate. They also learn other things about Japan, its society and its people.

Very strict with money and time, very hardworking. The mothers agree that the Japanese are very strict with money and that they do not give away money for no reason at all. Money has to be for some useful thing or activity. One mother says that the Japanese are so particular with accounting for money that one has to produce a receipt even for a five-centavo expense. The mothers do not like such strictness with money.

On the other hand, Vina, one of them, says that she learned how to save because of the Japanese example of making every centavo count. According to her, the Japanese like to save for a rainy day. She says that Filipinos are by nature "one-day millionaires" and when a Filipino has money, he likes to "sit pretty."

The mothers are one in saying that the Japanese are very strict with time. According to them, for the Japanese, a deadline is really a deadline. The Japanese are very hardworking. One says that she has seen them work late into the night.

The mothers have mixed attitudes toward Japanese industry. One says that the Japanese are really dedicated to their work; they do not just stop working when they feel like it, and they do not seem to get tired. She thinks such a trait is admirable. Another one says that if only Filipinos were as industrious as the Japanese, there would be no hunger in the Philippines. She says that the Filipinos can also be industrious but Japanese industry is a different kind. She adds that Filipinos are prone to gambling and oftentimes prioritize it over other activities.

On the other hand, the mothers (including the one who admires the hardworking Japanese) are unanimous in saying that the Japanese are too serious. Upon being asked to illustrate what this means, they say the Japanese are too industrious. When asked for a concrete example, they say that being industrious is connected with the use of money and time; they do not take a break from work and sometimes do not eat lunch. Such a practice once became a source of conflict. One mother relates that during one of their long meetings that went beyond lunchtime without food, one of the mothers suggested that *merienda* (snacks) at the very least should have been served. One of the Japanese staff members got upset and asked why the mothers were only after snacks. This made the mother angry because the imputation was not true at all; so she let the Japanese staff know that she was very mad. The staff apologized.[6]

Being too serious is also connected with lack of humor on the part of the Japanese. The mothers say the Japanese should learn to be less serious and be more appreciative of the jokes that the mothers make.

They mean what they say. The mothers also say that the Japanese mean what they say. According to one mother, the Japanese keep their word—they really do what they promise to do. One of the mothers says that it is "also good" (*OK din*) that the Japanese mean what they say because the mothers are learning to discipline themselves. She adds that when she thinks about the things she does not like about the Japanese, she realizes that in the greater scheme of things, it is all for the good. In other words, this mother has reservations about the strict adherence of the Japanese to what they say; however, although she initially disapproved of this behavior, after thinking about it she realized that it is a good source of personal discipline.

They are a source of inspiration. Since the Japanese staff is composed mostly of women, the mothers also see from their example that women can do much and that it is not only husbands but also wives who can work. Thus, for them, the Japanese staff is a source of inspiration because they have learned to work very hard and are able to do much as women. Vina adds that the Japanese staff members treat the mothers well although they have no education to speak of. She really appreciates that and this is why she feels good being with them.

Very fair. They say that the Japanese are fair in dealing with everyone in that they do not take sides when there are conflicts. Instead, they help resolve the conflicts by looking at the situation from all angles. Also, according to one mother, the Japanese do not play favorites in that when they give, they give to everyone, not just some.

Sincere and concerned. The mothers say that the Japanese are very sincere in their desire to help. One mother says that one can easily spot insincere people but the Japanese are really sincere and they really look after the welfare of the community and are trying to raise the quality of the mothers' lives. She laments the fact that her own government is not able to help or support them while people from another country are able to. She asks why it had to take another country to discover their skills and appreciate their products.

One of the mothers feels that the heart of the Japanese staff is really with them. According to her, the mothers have also learned to be concerned about others and that the Japanese staff members are their source of inspiration.

The mothers also feel that the Japanese are concerned about each one of them. One mother says that they always ask her about her health. Another mother says that when they visit, the Japanese would always ask how she has been, talk to her and ask her about her problems, her children, about anything in her life. The mothers say that the Japanese staff members eat with them and listen to their stories.

Unable to handle adversity as well as Filipinos. One of the mothers thinks that the Japanese staff does not have as much strength as the Filipino staff in terms of handling pressure. In fact, though it has not happened among ICAN's staff, she has heard that the Japanese even kill themselves when they no longer know what to do.

THE FILIPINO STAFF SPEAKS

This section discusses the perceptions of all three Filipino staff of ICAN. Maritess "Ate Tez" Estabillo-Cangao works as a program development officer; Marlyn "Mayen" Andes-Jamora is a project officer for the Education Program of ICAN; and Mariditha "Madet" Mondas is the health and nutrition officer of ICAN (interview, January 2007). Unlike the mothers, they are not recipients of aid from ICAN but rather coworkers, despite the fact that some of the ICAN staff members are the superiors of the Filipino staff. Moreover, having a higher level of education than the mothers, the Filipino staff of ICAN possesses different and richer concepts with which to express their impressions. But while the words are different, not all the concepts are different from those of the mothers.

They value honesty and trust. According to the Filipino staff, the Japanese value honesty very much. In connection with this, the Japanese emphasize trust so much so that if one does something wrong, or fails to do something that he/she promised, he/she cannot regain their trust anymore.

The staff members say they have learned to be true to their word. When they make a promise, they now know that they had better be able to live up to it and be responsible for it. For instance, Ate Tez says that if they make a proposal and promise that they will be able to get volunteers for a certain activity, they had better produce the volunteers.

The Filipino staff has also learned that trust is really very important. They have learned that the Japanese do not talk to people in whom they have lost trust, unlike Filipinos who still make small talk with people they know cannot be trusted.

They are disciplined when it comes to the budget. The Filipino staff says that the Japanese staff members are so disciplined regarding work and budgeting that when they say this budget is for a particular item, the Japanese staff really means it and one cannot use this money for any other item.

The Japanese are kuripot (stingy). The Filipino staff members are made to account for everything, up to the last centavo and, sometimes they have to use their own money. Ate Tez says that even the funds for the children's Christmas party in Payatas had to be sourced from solicitations. Ate Tez says that it seems that the principle of the Japanese staff is not to spend for the staff, only for the program. She says they did not even have an office Christmas party. They just joined the communities in Payatas who held their own party. According to Mayen and Madet the community also thinks that the Japanese are kuripot.

According to the Filipino staff, the Japanese do not adhere to the idea that when one gathers people for meetings, one has to feed them or give them snacks. Sometimes, they do not even eat lunch. They just work and work and continue with the meeting.

According to Madet, the Japanese seem to have the idea that if a person is a volunteer, he/she is not supposed to receive any incentive, not even snacks. But, she says, the Japanese staff has to understand that the people in Payatas do not have money and that ICAN is eating up their time with the meetings.

The Filipino staff member says they have learned to be honest, not that they were dishonest before. They explain that they have learned to be more careful and to really make an accounting of the budget up to the last centavo.

They are workaholics, too serious. The Filipino staff says the Japanese staff really like to work and are very dedicated. Mayen says that the Japanese work ethic is admirable. According to Madet, the Japanese like to do overtime work and when they work, they are really focused: no idle conversations. The Filipino staff says the Japanese are very strict with deadlines. When there is a deadline to meet, it is really a deadline.

According to Ate Tez, the Japanese panic easily when the deadline for an order (of the products the mothers make) is fast approaching and the Filipinos have not done a significant part of the work, even though the order was placed about three months before. But of course, Ate Tez explains, Filipinos like to do things at the last minute and so the mothers start working on the order only two weeks or so before the deadline. She says the Japanese staff then panic, thinking that the deadline will not be met, while the Filipinos are relaxed because they know it will be met. Ate Tez says that the Japanese used to be very strict with time schedules but have now learned to relax.

They are too serious and business-oriented. According to Madet, Filipino NGO workers tend to spend a lot of time on leisurely conversations in the communities as a way of building rapport but when the Japanese staff go down to the community they just talk about the project. It must be remembered, however, that the mothers say otherwise, that the Japanese talk to them about things outside of work, and the mothers like them for this.

Being too serious is also mentioned in the context of not seeing the value of going out of town for planning and bonding. The Japanese just do the planning in the office and even bring their own lunch. According to Madet, when they have training sessions, they are purely for training. In contrast, she says, Filipinos like to combine business and pleasure.

The Filipino staff thinks that the Japanese are sometimes insensitive to the fact that not all people are as workaholic as they are. Mayen and Madet think they are very serious while Filipinos on the other hand are more relaxed. Mayen says that Filipinos can still laugh even if the laptop crashes. For Tez, it has been a challenge working with the Japanese because of their workaholic attitude. She says she is still trying to discover how things work inside the Japanese mind.

They treat the Filipino staff as equals. According to the Filipino staff, the Japanese believe that each one has a potential, so they do not look down on other people or dismiss them as having no potential. The Filipinos feel good because they are treated as equals.

According to Mayen, the Japanese are not bossy at all. They even seem embarrassed when they ask the Filipinos to do things despite the fact that they are the boss. In fact, according to Madet, the Filipino staff can also ask the Japanese staff, including the Japanese executive director, to do things and run errands.

Open to ideas. The Japanese staff often ask the Filipinos questions about how things work, especially in the community. Tez says the Japanese are too humble to admit that they do not know much about many things and that they are willing to learn. This openness, according to Tez, makes the Filipinos feel that they are free to voice out complaints and suggestions. For instance, Madet thought that one Japanese was "*mataray*" (aloof and snobbish). So she told her and their Japanese boss about it. Now, this Japanese is aware of the impression that she gives to people in the office and in Payatas and tries to be more approachable.

Simple lifestyle. The Filipino staff admire the Japanese staff for dressing simply and working silently without much fanfare. Ate Tez cites the lack of an airconditioner in the office as a sign of their simplicity.

Committed. The Filipino staff think that the Japanese have a commitment to community service. According to Ate Tez, when the Japanese say they will stay with the community for ten years, they will really remain there for ten years. She says that they will not leave anyone hanging and just disappear or stop working in the middle of things.

On the other hand, Japanese easily get discouraged and when discouraged they leave their job. Madet says that when their plans do not go well they resign. A case in point is a former Japanese staff member who resigned because his plans did not work. She says that they easily back out when faced with what they think is a failure. Madet says that she has heard that they commit *harakiri* when they fail.

Respectful of Filipino culture and ways of doing things. Ate Tez is happy to observe that the Japanese are very respectful and aware that they are in the Philippines and have to do things as Filipinos do. For instance, she says that when the Japanese are offered something to eat, they will eat, or if they are offered an alcoholic drink, they will drink until they get drunk.

According to Ate Tez, when Madet has difficulty with a particular activity, the Japanese staff do not cut her out of the picture. Instead, they listen to her explanation without insisting on the Japanese way of doing things. According to Ate Tez, the Japanese staff might tell the Filipino staff how they do particular things in Japan but they do not insist on it. She says that the Japanese are willing to try other ways of doing things and are very respectful of the other's culture in that way.

Language barrier. In the Filipinos' opinion, one of the biggest weaknesses of the Japanese is that they are restricted in their movements and actions because of the language and cultural barrier. According to Madet, because the Japanese staff does not know the nuances of the Tagalog language that well yet, they often sound very straightforward when talking to the mothers in Tagalog and sometimes they sound offensive. The Filipino staff says this is really a weakness of the Japanese staff especially when it comes to organizing in the depressed communities like Payatas, where people tend to be very sensitive because of their poverty.

Individualistic. Madet thinks that Filipinos are better at teamwork. She says that the Japanese tend to work by themselves.

THE JAPANESE STAFF SPEAKS

In this section, the study explores the Japanese side of the relationship through one-on-one interviews with three Japanese staff members. The three interviewees are Nomura Yuki, ICAN executive director (interview, January 2007), Morisaki Yuki, ICAN program coordinator (interview, December 2006), and Suzuki Maho, volunteer intern nurse (ibid.).

One of the things that the Japanese admire and learned from the Filipinos is empowerment. All three Japanese staff members remark on how they have been empowered by the mothers. Nomura says that the mothers have given her strength while Morisaki talks about being empowered unexpectedly by the poor whom she had thought were powerless. Before, there were all kinds of categories in her mind—rich and poor, donor-donee, donor-recipients, powerful and powerless. But once she got to work with the people in Payatas, she realized that there really are no categories and that the labels are useless. In fact, she thinks that the poor have empowered her. Suzuki on the other hand talks about being inspired (*hagemasareta*) by the mothers and she writes about it in her blogs.

This empowerment is brought about by the Filipinos' unwavering optimism and tolerance of hardship. For instance, Morisaki says that the mothers in Payatas are "*masaya*" (happy) in spite of their poverty, while Suzuki says they are "*genki*" (cheerful, high-spirited or energetic). According to Morisaki, the Filipino mothers are always hopeful and positive and never say "no" to challenges. They are always "*kayang-kaya natin yan!*" (We can do it!). She thinks that the atmosphere is positive in spite of the dirty surroundings. The mothers inspire Nomura because they are very strong in the face of economic and family problems. They have a very unusual tolerance for hardships ("tolerance power"), Nomura says.

They greatly admire the Filipinos' sense of community. Nomura is amazed because there are many people who are really willing to work and serve the community. She relates that in a workshop with Japanese students on a study tour, the Japanese students were amazed at the mothers who not only live for themselves or their families but also for the community. She says it is something that the students cannot forget.

Also, the Japanese staff, especially Morisaki, admire the close family ties among Filipinos. She says the Filipino mothers like to say, "*Wala mang ulam pero basta magkasama, masaya na.*" (Even if we do not have food, as long as we are together, we are happy.) Although Morisaki has a good family, she is still envious of the *nanays* (mothers) in Payatas who value their families.

They also admire the warmth of the Filipino people. Suzuki, in particular, says she does not feel lonely among them because of such warmth. She likes the Filipinos because they are very friendly. When she arrived here, many talked to her immediately. They said to her,

"Your baby is very cute." She says that when she goes back to Japan she will honestly tell her friends that Payatas is very dirty and dangerous but many of its people are very friendly, unlike the Japanese, who do not display such warmth at *shoutaimen* (the first meeting).

The Japanese staff also admires the Filipinos because they are very patient and "*masipag*" (hardworking). Both Morisaki and Nomura mention Madet, the Filipino nurse, who caught TB because she was always with sick people.

Inevitably, the Japanese get to reflect on their own society. Morisaki, while admitting that she may be making a hasty generalization, talks about how the people in Japan, unlike the Filipinos, seem to get easily depressed, an observation that Suzuki confirms from her medical work experience in Japan. Suzuki says that although the Japanese people have money and education, many suffer from depression. Morisaki thinks that in this sense it is really the Japanese people who are poor, not the Filipinos.

The Health Assistance and Neighborhood Development Support (HANDS)

HANDS was founded by Yamazaki Tomiko on 1 July 1996 and was registered as an NPO in the Kanagawa Prefecture on 12 October 2000. Its aim is to provide support to indigenous peoples and make them self-reliant and self-sufficient in their communities. The immediate stimulus for the founding of HANDS was the personal experience of the founder, who developed a stomach ache and the flu while visiting a community of indigenous peoples. It was then that she felt very helpless because there were no doctors. She realized that it must be very difficult for the people to get sick and not be given expert medical care.

The Japanese staff looks at HANDS as a "very small" NGO. It has 200 paying members. There are four part-time staff members in Japan who do not get salaries but only an honoraria. In other words, they are part-time, unsalaried, volunteer staff. HANDS has no office here in the Philippines but it has one Japanese staff member in Marbel, General Santos city, who apparently plans to stay there permanently.

Unlike ICAN, which works with the community, the involvement of HANDS is less direct. It has partners instead with local NGOs or Cooperatives. HANDS is responsible for raising resources in Japan, while the local NGOs are responsible for the implementation of projects in the communities. The partnerships with the Cooperative of Women in Health and Development (COWHED) and the Partnership for First Peoples (PFP) are the focus of this case study on HANDS.[7] COWHED is based in Lake Sebu in South Cotabato and works with T'boli women, while PFP operates among indigenous people in Sultan Kudarat, including the Manobos in B'lakul.

The B'lakul Community Assesses HANDS

This section discusses how the communities perceive the HANDS projects. For the assessment of the projects in B'lakul, a focus group discussion (FGD) was held with the members of the Board of Trustees of the Manobo-T'boli of B'lakul Community Association, Incorporated or MTBCAI (FGD, 27 December 2006). A separate interview with its president and a conversation with one of the scholarship recipients of HANDS who now teaches in the B'lakul Community School were also conducted (FGD, 28 December 2006).

Support for the salaries of teachers. In B'lakul, a school was built with the help of another JNGO, Friends of Tribals (FOT). HANDS now gives financial support for the salary of the schoolteachers in the elementary school. It gives about 16,000 to 17,000 pesos a month which, together with the contributions from the students, support five teachers. (The students are required to pay 35 pesos a month, but since not all can pay, the contributions are practically voluntary.) HANDS' support of the school is, for the community, the most significant assistance from that organization because it ensures the continuous operation of their school which for them is the "best" project that ever came to their community, thanks to FOT.

It is also a matter of pride for them that the school continues to operate. They said that before, it was they who went down the mountain—one hour away on foot—and studied in the school of the "Kristiyanos" (literally, Christians, but the word is used to refer to all lowlanders), and felt like outsiders. But now, it is the Kristiyanos who come to their school to study.

Most importantly, one of the members of the focus group thinks that without the school, the community might have already disappeared, like other Manobo communities, as they each try to find their luck wherever fate brings them. But because of the school, they have a very good reason to stay in the community, since the running of the school gives the community something to do, and a reason for being together.

College scholarships. HANDS gives scholarships to Manobo students who want to get a bachelor's degree or vocational training. It pays for the whole semester which costs 17,000 pesos in tuition and allowances as well as food, board and lodging since the grantees will have to leave the community and live in the city.

Six Manobo students have already graduated from college as teachers through the scholarships given by HANDS. They came back to teach in their own community school and ensure the sustainability of the school. There are now three more who are studying to get their bachelor's degree in Education.

Livelihood projects. HANDS financed the planting of fruit trees which the community hopes will become an alternative to cash crop farming as a source of income. It also financed the goat-raising program. According to the FGD participants, the fruit trees have not yet actually benefited them because it takes time for the trees to grow. But they hope that in the future, the trees will become viable alternative sources of income since corn farming, their main source of livelihood at present, is not that profitable anymore. On the other hand, the twenty-one goats distributed to the families for breeding have now multiplied to forty-nine as of last count.

Water system. The community also recently got a potable water system with the financial and human resource assistance of HANDS.

The water system has been a great help for the community. They are happy that they now have safe and clean water. They used to get water from a well or a spring that turned murky when it rained. Now the water source is encased in a concrete tank and does not get dirty or murky anymore. Thus, water-borne diseases have been avoided. Also, because of the pipes, water has been brought closer to the families who used to hike to the spring to get water.

The COWHED Members Assess the Projects

The only HANDS project in Lake Sebu is livelihood support to T'boli women in the cooperative. The support comes in the form of capitalization for the cooperative, administrative support, and marketing of its products such as t'nalak, traditional beads, and embroidered clothes sold in trade fairs. To assess the assistance of HANDS to COWHED in Lake Sebu, two T'boli women were interviewed.

Maria is a beads-maker, separated from her husband for four years now, and has ten children. She makes most of the beaded accessories that COWHED sells—necklaces, earrings, headdresses and other beaded products (interview, 28 December 2006). The income that she gets from the sale of her beads to COWHED, though not enough for her large family, goes a long way towards feeding her children and sending some of them to school.

As an ambulant vendor Maria earns 100 to 150 pesos a day. However, she works only four days a month on the average. Since she became a member of COWHED, she has earned a monthly income of around 1,000 pesos per day on top of her 100 to 150 pesos per day as an ambulant vendor.

Although the 1000 pesos she earns as producer for COWHED is not enough to feed her big family, she is very grateful because at least her income is more stable than what she gets as an ambulant vendor. This is made possible by the fact that COWHED obviously has a bigger market outside of Lake Sebu. She is also the priority of COWHED among all the producers because of her economic circumstances.

Maria is happy that she became a member of COWHED because it gives cash advances which she uses as capital to produce the beads and which sometimes become her source of emergency funds for her family's needs. She says that these cash advances have been a great help to her.

Aside from this purely economic benefit, she is also given the chance to go to other places whenever COWHED is invited to participate in trade fairs. She feels a sense of accomplishment as part of a trade fair. She entertains customers, gives them sales talk, and chats with customers to convince them to buy the products ready for sale, as well as to take orders.

Hilda, a *t'nalak* weaver, is one of the founding members of COWHED. She is a mother of six (interview, 29 December 2006). According to her, t'nalak weaving is the main source of income for her family since she earns more than her husband, a farmer. Although some of Hilda's children are working now, she does not ask them for money. In fact, it is she who gives them money.

Hilda is very grateful that she is a member of COWHED, through which she gets most of her orders. Without the income from her t'nalak weaving, she would not be able to support her family. She earns about 750 pesos per month.

She appreciates the help HANDS gives to the women of COWHED and she feels loved by them. She is proud that her products are being sold in Japan by HANDS.

Perceptions of Key Persons in the Filipino Partner Organizations

Three staff members from the local partner NGOs of HANDS were interviewed. The two from PFP are Rony Subibe (executive director) and Noe "Nono" Lamanero (project director/project development officer); the one from COWHED is Melchie Uyasan (chairperson). The three interviewees representing the local NGO partners of HANDS share many common perceptions of the HANDS staff.

Sincerity and commitment. First, the three Filipinos agree that the sincerity and commitment of HANDS is unquestionable. The interviewees from PFP say that the visit of the HANDS staff members to the communities in spite of the risk to their lives is a proof of their commitment (interview, 29 December 2006). For Melchie the suggestions given to COWHED to improve their operations and make their products more marketable are proof of the staff's sincerity and concern.

For both the PFP and COWHED staff, the commitment of the HANDS staff members is also best seen in how they keep their promises, which to Nono, is the badge of professionalism. This is also something that came out in the interviews with the B'lakul community.

Trust. The three interviewees mention trust as something very important in their relationship with HANDS. In fact, they say, this Japanese emphasis on trust has implications on the manner in which they deal with the Filipinos and how the Filipinos deal with them, a manner that is different from the way the Filipinos deal with other partners they have had.

For instance, in the case of COWHED which does not even have any written contract or memorandum of agreement (MOA) with HANDS, Melchie says that because she and the women in COWHED feel trusted, they see to it that they live up to such trust; thus, they wholeheartedly and sincerely deliver more than they would otherwise do. She says that for her, trust, more than any written contract or agreement, builds real responsibility.

Nono calls it the "Japanese way." Thus, when the Filipinos make project proposals, they make sure that they touch the hearts of the Japanese. They do not just rattle off statistics and figures like they do in submitting proposals to other foreign NGOs. They present HANDS with actual cases and situations of people who experience poverty. Nono thinks that this "different mindset" must also be the reason why HANDS visits the communities and looks at the real situation.

All the interviewees agree that, in effect, they are able to make proposals that are really needs-based and address situations in the grassroots. For Melchie, this makes HANDS more relevant to the grassroots than the other NGOs she has worked with where the neediest are often disqualified from the projects because of the documentary requirements. For Nono, this is one reason why HANDS and PFP feel very comfortable with each other.

Reflections of Japanese NGO staff

According to Yamazaki, most of the members of HANDS are senior citizens, the average age being sixty. Many of them experienced the horrors of the Second World War and remember their difficult lives before as children during and after the war. So they understand the experience of poor children in the Philippines now.

Some of their members, on the other hand, feel some guilt over what Japan did to Asian countries, particularly the Philippines during the Second World War. They know that Japanese soldiers made the Filipinos suffer and they want to make amends, which is why they joined HANDS. Some old people see their contribution to HANDS as compensation for what the Japanese did during the Second World War.

Simplicity. Yamazaki says that Japan is rich and the people live affluent lifestyles. Because of that, Japan uses too much energy and resources. It is wasteful. She therefore believes that the Japanese must learn to live simply and to value simplicity, like the Filipinos.

Aida Yoko, the Japanese staff of HANDS staying at Marbel, hopes that the indigenous peoples will be satisfied with their lives at present. She says that she moved to Hokkaido from Tokyo because she did not like the urban life which lays too much stress on money. She does not think economic development is everything. Looking at the children in Japan now, she thinks they are not brought up as human beings. Japan has failed in this respect, but not many Japanese think that way. She therefore does not want the Filipinos to emulate the Japanese. The indigenous peoples have their own way of life and they should be proud of it, she says. She does not think that the JNGOs like HANDS should impose their ways as the only means to improvement or development.

Exploitation. And where does Japan get its energy and resources? Yamazaki says that although technically Japan does not steal the resources of poor countries, in reality it does because it buys these natural resources to support its affluent lifestyle and, this is a form of exploitation.

As a former high-school geography teacher she knows very well that because of its topography, Japan does not have a lot of natural resources. That is why it has to import products like lumber and coal from neighboring Asian countries, including the Philippines. As a result, the mountains become denuded, thus affecting the indigenous people who live there and who depend on such resources.

Yamazaki also relates that after the Second World War, Japan improved economically by exploiting the resources of other countries. She says that exploitation continues up to now, and it can be said that Japan lives because of other people like the Filipinos. The Japanese people ought to realize this: they should know how to be global citizens, to feel guilty, and at the same time thankful for their prosperity.

Synthesis and Conclusion

ICAN and HANDS are not cultural JNGOs. Their primary goal is to help in the improvement of the economic lives of the people in Payatas and the indigenous peoples, respectively. And yet, because of the person-to-person interactions in the process of working toward their goals, both Japanese and Filipinos gain awareness of each other's values and ways of doing things.

The chapter has shown that, depending on how immersed NGOs are in the community, person-to-person interactions result in volumes of knowledge about each other. ICAN is more immersed in Payatas than HANDS is among the indigenous people. As a result, the members of ICAN seem to be more knowledgeable about Payatas and its poor than the members of HANDS are about the indigenous peoples. The same thing can be said about the poor of Payatas and the indigenous peoples vis-à-vis ICAN and HANDS, respectively.

The awareness of each other's values and ways of doing things is more visible in the case of ICAN because it is immersed in Payatas. The awareness is less in the case of HANDS because its members do not regularly visit the indigenous peoples—their interaction is more with the local NGOs than with the community itself.

The limited awareness of the indigenous peoples' values and culture in the case of HANDS can be detected in the limited comments the Japanese interviewees are able to express about the indigenous peoples. Most of their comments are actually about Japan (affluent life, exploitation of Asia, Second World War hardships of the Japanese and Japanese atrocities in Asia, etc.) rather than about the values and culture of the indigenous peoples. Likewise, the peoples of B'lakul and Lake Sebu have little to say about the Japanese beyond what the Japanese are doing (helping them get an education, visiting them, etc.). The same thing can be said about the members of the local NGO partners of HANDS. Their comments about the sincerity of the Japanese and the value they put on trust are more of comments about procedures in making project proposals, rather than comments on the Japanese as a people.

This is in contrast to the perceptions of the Payatas community, which is able to say that the Japanese are *kuripot*, strict with time, individualistic, have no sense of humor, hardworking, disciplined, fair, honest, open to ideas, committed, lead a simple life at least while in the community or in the office, have respect for local culture and ways of doing things. The staff members of ICAN, likewise, have much to say about the Filipinos they have interacted with: they are a source of empowerment, optimistic, possess a sense of community, have strong family ties, are patient and hardworking.

Findings of the research show that the creation of impressions and of feelings (like or dislike) is a two-way process, but they cannot be measured: There is no definite answer to the question of whether the Filipinos are more influenced by the Japanese, or vice-versa. In the case of ICAN, the mothers admire Japanese industry, but are not prepared to be as workaholic as the Japanese. In fact, they seem to take pride in their observation that the Japanese have learned from them how to relax and mix business with pleasure. This is only one example of mutual influence, but the research design is limited in that it cannot list all the influences which are mutual and otherwise. Findings in the case of HANDS are more inconclusive because the comments of both the Filipino and Japanese interviewees are scanty and do not directly touch on cultural influences.

Nonetheless, the findings show that person-to-person interactions not only prevent the creation of extreme impressions and stereotypes, but also produce mixed impressions —negative and positive. As mentioned in the beginning of this paper, closer and more frequent interactions between the Filipinos and the Japanese have helped Filipinos to form a more balanced view of Japan.

Notes

1. For instance, in explaining why the Japanese government gradually encouraged emigration to the Philippines in the 1900s, Jose cited two reports, one published in 1909 by the Japanese Ministry of Agriculture and Commerce where it was observed that Filipinos were "friendly and hospitable" to the Japanese and "had respect and affection for them" and another one reported in 1911 by Vice-Consul Iwatani Jokichi where it was said that the non-Christian Filipinos were friendly to the Japanese and that the former were grateful that the Japanese were cultivating the lands in Mindanao (Jose 1998, 290). Here, it can be clearly seen that indeed people-to-people relations and how the Japanese and the Filipinos view each other on the personal level are important components of bilateral relations and were even considered by officials in making official reports.

2. According to the JANIC 1994 Directory, of the 166 Japanese NGOs with activities in Asia and the Oceania, fifty were in the Philippines, the highest presence in any one country (Menju 1996, 154).

3. The presentation itself did not give the reasons why the Philippines is the most popular destination for JNGOs. The reason was clarified only when the presenters responded to the author's query during the open forum.

4. Between 1907 and 1917, 37 percent of all Japanese in Southeast Asia were in the Philippines. This steadily rose to 63.7 percent in 1940 (Jose 1998, 292).

5. At present, OISCA has several projects spread all over the Philippines: Nueva Vizcaya, Abra, Negros Occidental, Quezon, Compostela Valley, Palawan and Zamboanga del Norte (OISCA 2002, 36–39).

6. According to the author's Japanese friend who works in the Embassy of Japan in Manila, the Filipino staff of the embassy have the same complaint about long meetings and snacks not being served.

7. The other partners are Catholic Mission for Indigenous Peoples (CMIP) and Pasasambao Integrated Health Services. CMIP in General Santos City works among the B'laans while Pasasambao works with the Sangils also in General Santos. Pasasambao is headed by Mrs. Napsa Sara whose sister, Aga, is married to a Japanese and is now living in Japan. Yamazaki knows her sister Aga in Japan who told the former about Pasasambao. Their work with Pasasambao is to upgrade a Moro community.

References

Focus group discussion, 27 December 2006, B'lakul, Sultan Kudarat.

JANIC (Japanese NGO Center for International Cooperation).1996. *Directory of Japanese NGOs*. http://www.janic.org/en/directoryof japanesengos.html. Viewed 11 August 2007.

The Japan Times. 5 November 2002.

Jose, Lydia N. Yu. 1998. "Philippines-Japan Relations: The Revolutionary Years and a Century Hence." In *Philippine External Relations: A Centennial Vista,* ed. Baviera, Aileen San Pablo, and Lydia N. Yu Jose. Manila: Foreign Service Institute.

_______. 2000. "Japan: Curio, Enemy, Inspiration, Model, and Now?" In *Philippines and Japan: Directions and Challenges,* ed. Lydia N. Yu Jose, and Rosalina Palanca Tan. Quezon City: Japanese Studies Program, Ateneo de Manila University.

_______. 2005. " The Politics of an Economic Partnership." In *Asian Cooperation: Problems and Challenges in the New Century*. Quezon City: Ateneo Center for Asian Studies.

Menju Toshihiro. 1996. "The Evolution of Japanese NGOs in the Asia Pacific Context." In *Emerging Civil Society in the Asia Pacific Community*, ed. Yamamoto Tadashi. Tokyo: Japan Center for International Exchange.

OISCA. 2002. Annual Report, FY 2001(April 2001–March 2002). Tokyo: OISCA-International.

"Philippines-Japan NGO Symposium." 2006. Market! Market!, Bonifacio Global City, Taguig City. 24 November.

INTERVIEWS

Hilda. 2006. Lake Sebu, South Cotabato. 29 December.

Maria. 2006. Lake Sebu, South Cotabato. 28 December.

Maritess. 2007. "Ate Tez" Estabillo-Cangao. KFC, Teacher's Village, Quezon City. 19 January.

Mariditha "Madet" Mondas. 2007. KFC, Teacher's Village, Quezon City. 19 January.

Marlyn "Mayen" Andes-Jamora. 2007. KFC, Teacher's Village, Quezon City. 19 January.

Melchie Uyasan. 2006. Lake Sebu, South Cotabato. 28 December.

Morisaki Yuki. 2006. McDonald's, Teacher's Village, Quezon City. 7 December.

Noe "Nono" Lamero. 2006. PFP Office, South Cotabato. 29 December.

Nomura Yuki. 2007. KFC, Teacher's Village, Quezon City. 11 January.

Rony Subibe. 2006. PFP Office, South Cotabato. 29 December.

Rowena Baltazar. 2007. ICAN Community Care Center, Payatas, Quezon City. 24 January.

Shirley Naag. 2007. ICAN Community Care Center, Payatas, Quezon City. 24 January.

Suzuki, Maho. 2006. Mocha Blends, Teacher's Village, Quezon City. 7 December.

Vina Cardama. 2007. ICAN Community Care Center, Payatas, Quezon City. 24 January.

Conclusion

We have focused on people rather than on trade, investments, and loans because in the bilateral relations between the Philippines and Japan, it is the movement of peoples across the national borders of these two states and the people-to-people relations that have been thick and sustained through the centuries. People-to-people relations call for a more serious attention, especially now that thousands of Filipino migrant workers go to Japan every year. Furthermore, there are definite plans to send Filipino caregivers and nurses to Japan. They will be engaged in an occupation that involves an intimate encounter with foreign cultures—both for the Filipino caregivers/nurses and the Japanese patients—an encounter that is sure to affect both sides culturally.

In focusing on people, we did not undermine the importance of economic relations between the Philippines and Japan. On the contrary, we took off from that assumption. Moreover, in focusing on people, we did not neglect the official diplomatic relations between the two countries. And last but not least, we did not focus on migration itself, but rather, on cross-cultural interactions.

The following are our observations:

Japan's economic and cultural policies concerning the Philippines in the 1950s through the 1970s were difficult to implement because of the Filipino people's memories of the past, especially of the Japanese occupation of the Philippines. As the relations mature, the Philippine government has tended to brush aside the past, and focus more on friendship and cooperation with Japan. This is a practical move because the Philippine government wishes to attract more Japanese investments, loans, and tourists to the country. The memories of the past, however, will not go away, for monuments and markers about them have become part of the Philippine physical landscape. Many have even become tourist attractions. Moreover, the Japanese occupation is part of history lessons in Philippine primary schools and is usually the source of the Japanese popular image, as seen in the plots of some Filipino movies even to this date. It is unlikely that Filipino intellectuals and the mass media will constantly point to the Japanese occupation as an example of what the Japanese are like and what harm they did—this portrayal of the Japanese was typical in the 1950s and 1960s. However, although the portrayal is no longer as harsh, there is no guarantee that it will never be repeated.

The conclusion of Chapter 2 about the intertwining relationship between economics and cultural influences is confirmed in the other chapters. The Japanese Studies Program in Ateneo did not get under way until the 1980s because there were almost no job opportunities for graduates with sufficient knowledge of Japan and the Japanese language. The Ateneo was not willing to invest time and money in such a program. This policy conflicted with the desire of the Japan Foundation to transfer to the university the financial burden of supporting the program's faculty and staff within the agreed time frame. One can speculate that if the financial support from the Japanese government had no limit, many of the problems related to the status of the program could have been avoided. However, this would not necessarily be so because of the plain fact that students study to prepare for a career or a job; they do not take a course simply because it is available for free.

On the other hand, cultural interest is not always connected with the calculation of monetary gain. Ateneo maintained the Japanese

Studies Program even after the Japan Foundation stopped the salary support to the faculty and the sending of visiting professors. It was maintained, of course, according to what the university deemed practical, given the lack of interest among the general student body. This indicates that the Ateneo appreciated the importance of maintaining an academic link with Japan. The exchange program between Ateneo and Sophia professors of Mathematics was initiated and maintained primarily because the Philippines needed more and better teachers of Mathematics, and Ateneo wanted to meet this need. The professors from Sophia were willing to participate in the program perhaps because of the new experience it offered and the chance to broaden their horizons through joint projects with people from a different culture. The financial assistance from the Japan Society for the Promotion of Science (JSPS) only reinforced the mutual interests that were already there. The same thing can be said about the Japan Information and Cultural Center (JICC). Despite the fact that its activities could be enjoyed free of charge, they hardly aroused any curiosity about Japan. Few Filipinos spent their time attending the cultural events sponsored by the JICC. And curiosity is usually the start of cross-cultural experiences.

More important than the money which supported these cultural activities were the people behind them. Certainly, some of the Filipinos who were involved ran into personal conflicts with some Japanese, but there were more stories of friendship and cooperation, as narrated in the stories about the Japanese Studies Program in Ateneo, the JICC, and the exchange program between Japanese and Filipino Mathematics professors. Indeed, the friendship that developed out of these cultural activities goes beyond the structure and even the lifetime of the institutional activities.

Since the 1980s, large groups of Filipinos, a great percentage of whom are migrant workers, have become part of the people-to-people interaction between the Philippines and Japan. With this development, which we may call the popularization of Philippines-Japan relations, the Japanese government's control of what aspects of Japanese culture to promote has been undermined. The JICC and the Japan Foundation always choose what they consider to be the desirable aspects of Japanese culture for promotion: ikebana, classical performing arts, Kurosawa movies, and the like. With the popularization of Philippines-Japan relations, the Filipinos and the Japanese make their choices. Cultural promotion is largely out of the hands of Japanese government agencies. It is now promoted by people, by mass media, and commercial Japanese goods for mass consumption.

Intercultural marriages between Filipinos and Japanese are just one of the results of the sizeable cross-border movement of peoples between the Philippines and Japan. Love, not necessarily money, has led to the exchange of cultural traits and practices; in some cases, one of the spouses may even give up certain aspects of his/her culture. Mutual understanding and the resolve to keep the marriage intact despite all odds is usually the catalyst for cultural change on the part of the spouses.

We subscribe to the commonly accepted observation that the Philippines-Japan relationship is unequal, but only in the sense that it is a relationship between a developed and a developing country. We tentatively accept the other common observation that it is primarily economic in nature. But, if possession of resources—human and natural—is taken into account, it is not easy to jump to the conclusion that in this unequal relationship, the Philippines has less and Japan has more. On the other hand, if only money is taken into account, Japan obviously has more and the Philippines has less.

Admitting conditionally that the Philippines-Japan relationship is unequal, we proceeded by asking under what circumstances it is unequal: in what cases does Japan carry more weight than the other? In what cases is it the other way around? Are there cases when the Philippines and Japan are perfectly equal?

It is true that with respect to financial resources, Japan has more than the Philippines. The Asian Development Bank, where Japan has the biggest share, is only one of the manifestations of this. Japan's capacity to offer scholarships and research grants to foreign students and professionals, to send visiting professors to the Philippines to teach about Japan, to support institutions like the Japan Information and Cultural Center and the Japan Foundation, which primarily aim at promoting Japanese culture abroad, and the presence of Japanese NGOs in the Philippines whose mission is to help develop the Philippines—all these are also manifestations. The most glaring evidence is the influx of Filipino migrant workers to Japan and the debts that the Philippines owes not only the Asian Development Bank but also other national and international financial institutions. Even in cases of intercultural marriages, more often than not it is the Japanese spouse, whether husband or wife, who is more financially endowed than the Filipino spouse.

A closer look at the list above, however, reveals a more complicated relationship. First of all, the list of things Japan is able to do because it is financially endowed is a mixture of activities that definitely need money, as well as activities that are more dependent on people and their attitude toward the activities. Scholarships, research grants, sending of visiting professors, activities of the Japan Information and Cultural Center and of the Japan Foundation, are dependent on the quantity and quality of people who participate. The Asian Development Bank and loans are clearly mainly financial. Activities of the Japanese NGOs in the Philippines and motivations and behavior of Filipino workers in Japan, on the other hand, are not solely measured by possession of money. They are a mixture of money, culture, and much more. To make matters more complicated, it may be pointed out that the cultural activities of Japan in the 1950s and 1960s were not totally unconnected to the ultimate aim of promoting Japanese trade and investment. This is not to deny that Japan has also practiced cultural diplomacy for its own sake and indeed, the cultural aim has become more obvious since the 1970s.

In conclusion, we identify history, love, and money, as conceptualized in the introduction, as the three major elements of Philippines-Japan relations after the Second World War. We revise the oft-repeated observation that Philippines-Japan relations are primarily economic. Having said that the movement of peoples between the Philippines and Japan is the thickest and most sustained activity in the bilateral relations, it would be tantamount to reducing these people to a status of economic goods if it were true that the bilateral relationship was primarily economic. We argue that Philippines-Japan relations are primarily about the past, love, and money. The past always hovers, although often unobtrusively, over the present relationship. Both love and money, or just one of them, may be found in a participant in the bilateral relations between the Philippines and Japan.

When history, love and money are taken together, Philippines-Japan relations cannot be simply described as unequal. Even if we grant that Japan's and the Philippines' goals are economic, both of them have to use cultural means to achieve their goals. And the historical past is part of culture. Japan vis-à-vis the Philippines tends to be hampered by its past history of aggression. When the Japanese side commits undesirable acts, usually the Philippine side can say "parang noong Panahon ng Hapon," "just like during the Japanese occupation." And the public understands what it means. But the Japanese side cannot say anything similar to criticize the Philippines. History can empower the Philippines, but not Japan.

Japanese have more money than Filipinos, generally speaking, but when their interactions are in the area of cultural exchange, the money that the Japanese have does not always give them the power to make the Filipinos do want they want. Usually, it is mutual adjustment to each side's goals and priorities, rather than money, that enables the two sides to arrive at a compromise.

When interactions between Japanese and Filipinos result in cultural influences, an interesting question is who influences whom more strongly? Simply put, which culture persists, which one gives in? We have seen in the chapters on intercultural marriages and Japanese NGOs that there are real cases of culture change. The chapters on these topics show that the Filipinos tend to influence the Japanese more in such matters as family relationships, relaxation, spiritual serenity, and gender equality, while the Japanese tend to have more influence in matters of cleanliness, discipline, and industry. In other words, both sides come out culturally richer.

Milestones, Steppingstones, Turning Points

*1956 July 23

The Philippine Senate ratifies the San Francisco Peace Treaty. Peaceful relations between the Philippines and Japan, broken by the Second World War and the Japanese occupation of the Philippines from 1941 to 1945, are thus restored. The reparations treaty between the two countries is also ratified.

It has taken Japan and the Philippines more than a decade to normalize relations after the Second World War because the two governments have to agree first on the terms of war reparations and security arrangements in the Asia Pacific, not to mention the still lingering antipathy towards Japan.

Thus, Philippines-Japan relations are officially restored in July 1956, but a lot of work remains to be done to make the relationship between the former wartime enemies smooth, mutually beneficial, and friendly.

---

†1956 August 8

The first Japanese goodwill mission, headed by Murata Shozo (Ambassador to the Japanese-sponsored Philippine Republic during the Japanese occupation), arrives in Manila. Composed of seventeen members, the mission makes a courtesy call on President Carlos P. Garcia, and enjoys a tour of Baguio City. The mission aims to explore ways and means of hastening the restoration of friendly relations between the Philippines and Japan.

§1956 November 18

The Association for Japan-Philippines Memorialization (Nippi Irei Kai) holds its inaugural meeting in Japan. Among the distinguished persons in attendance are the Philippine ambassador to Japan, the widows of executed Generals Yamashita Tomoyuki and Homma Masaharu (Yamashita Hisako and Homma Fujiko, respectively), officials of the Japanese ministries of foreign affairs and health, and influential Japanese personalities who were in the Philippines during or before the Second World War.

The association aims to hold a joint memorialization of the Japanese and Filipinos who saw action and died in the Philippines during the Second World War. Part of the memorialization is the sending of missions to the Philippines to gather the bones of the Japanese war dead. Thus, in January 1958, a delegation with such a mission arrives in Manila. A courtesy call is paid on President Carlos P. Garcia, who instructs all government agencies concerned to assist the mission. The Japanese government is wary that such a mission might meet antagonism in the Philippines. On the whole, the concern has proven baseless, but in some places visited by the mission, shouts of "bakayaro" (a Japanese curse word) are heard.

More bone-gathering missions and memorial services for the dead follow, reaching a peak around 1977.

† 1957 June 21

Republic Act Number 1789, "An Act Prescribing the National Policy in the Procurement and Utilization of Reparations and Development Loans from Japan, Creating a Reparations Commission to Implement the Policy, Providing Funds Therefore, and for Other Purposes," otherwise known as "The Reparations Law of 1957," is passed. The law stipulates that procurement of capital goods and services will be limited to those deemed advantageous to economic development and industrialization. Out of nine areas of development prioritized, the government is allowed to participate in four, namely, electrification, firefighting equipment, railways, and telecommunications.

The law is revised in June 1961. Among the revisions are: increase in reparations goods allocated for the government, provision for a bidding system for the private sector, repeal of the repayment grace period, requirement of full first-year payment upon delivery of the goods, and provision that projects should reflect availability of funds.

On 13 August 1971 the National Economic Council (NEC) decides to channel to the public sector the remaining balance of the reparations account amounting to US$175 million (out of the total US$550 million). The decision is soon overtaken by the declaration of martial law in September 1972, thus embroiling the implementation of the reparations law in huge cases of corrupt practices.

† 1958 December 1

President Carlos P. Garcia leaves for Tokyo to begin his five-day state visit. He addresses a joint session of the Japanese Diet, the first foreign head of government to do so. The Japanese Diet rules prohibit speeches by foreigners. To get around the rules, the occasion is presented as a welcome party by the two chambers of the Diet.

In a joint communiqué during the visit, the Japanese government agrees to extend a commercial loan for the construction of a multipurpose dam in Marikina and the modernization of the Philippine telecommunications system, using the reparations account as collateral. In addition, the Philippines and Japan agree to consider initiating negotiations at an appropriate time for a treaty of amity, commerce and navigation.

The multipurpose Marikina dam and the modernization of the telecommunications system are never realized due to several changes in the plans and priorities of the Philippine government. On the other hand, the Treaty of Amity, Commerce and Navigation, which Japan has been hoping for, will take close to two decades before it is finally ratified.

† 1962 November 5-10

Crown Prince Akihito and Princess Michiko, the present emperor and empress of Japan, visit the Philippines. It is commonly believed that the aim of the visit is to charm the Philippine government into ratifying the treaty of amity, commerce, and navigation.

* 1965 December 1

It is decided to establish the Asian Development Bank (ADB) in Manila. The decision is a diplomatic triumph for the Philippines over Japan, which, despite a vigorous campaign, fails in its bid to have the bank's headquarters in Tokyo. On 19 December 1966 the ADB is inaugurated.

† 1966 December 14

The first visiting Japanese professors arrive in Ateneo de Manila University. The following day, they begin to teach the following subjects: The Development of Japanese Economy, Postwar Development of Japanese Economy, and Japanese Language and culture. This is the beginning of the first Japanese Studies program in the Philippines, with support from the Japanese government.

On 24 February 1967 the Japanese Studies Program in Ateneo is formally and officially inaugurated. Cocktails are served and a documentary film on the visit of President Marcos to Japan is shown, followed by speeches of congratulations and gratitude by officials of the Japanese Embassy and the university.

† 1967 April 19

President Ferdinand Marcos, reversing the stand of previous presidents not to allow the entry of Japanese business into the Philippines, orders the Securities and Exchange Commission to entertain applications of Japanese nationals and corporations to do business in the Philippines. By the following year, fifteen Japanese trading firms have started operating in Manila: Mitsui, Mitsubishi, Nichimen, Marubeni, Sumitomo, Nissho, Toyo Menka, Ataka, Kanematsu-gosho, Iwai, Chori, Itoh, Nippi Boeki, Kowa, and Nomura Trading. Japan Air Lines has also started flying to the Philippines.

Due to an exposé of irregularities regarding the trading companies' permit to operate in the Philippines, the mayor of Manila orders their closure. Investigations of the exposé are begun but soon get buried in the excitement of the 1969 presidential election that will see the reelection of Marcos, the first Philippine president ever to be reelected.

† 1967 September 12

The Japan Information Center (JIC) opens in Manila. It later becomes the Japan Information and Cultural Center (JICC).

† 1972 January

Kishi Nobusuke, president of the Philippine Society of Japan (Firipin Kyokai), visits the Philippines to inaugurate the Philippines-Japan

Society. The Society, based in Manila and composed of Filipinos and Japanese, should not be confused with the Philippine Society of Japan, which is based in Japan and is composed of Japanese members only. At the inauguration, Kishi announces that a Japanese war memorial will be erected in Caliraya, Batangas.

*1973 MARCH 28

The Caliraya Memorial Park in Batangas province, the first large-scale war memorial built by the Japanese government on foreign land is inaugurated. The decision to build this memorial was made in June 1971 and was publicly announced by Kishi Nobusuke in January 1972 during the inaugural ceremony of the establishment of the Philippines-Japan Society.

*1973 DECEMBER 27

President Ferdinand Marcos declares the Treaty of Amity, Commerce and Navigation between the Philippines and Japan as ratified. The treaty was signed by the two governments on 9 December 1960; the Japanese Diet ratifies it on 31 October 1961. But the Philippine Senate withholds ratification for years. On 2 March 1972 the Philippine Senate rejects the resolution for the ratification of the treaty. Marcos declares martial law on 21 September of the same year, abolishes the Philippine Congress, and assumes absolute power. In his capacity as chief executive and lawmaker, he declares the treaty ratified in 1973. Instruments of ratification are exchanged between Foreign Affairs Secretary Carlos P. Romulo and Japanese Ambassador Urabe Toshio, after the exchange of diplomatic notes on a Japanese loan of seventeen million pesos to the Philippines.

The difficulty undergone by the treaty attests to the still lingering anti-Japanese sentiments because of the Second World War.

† 1974 JANUARY

Japanese Prime Minister Tanaka Kakuei visits the Philippines on the last leg of his official tour of Southeast Asian countries. He is met with student protests in all the countries he visits except the Philippines, which has been under martial law since September 1972.

§ 1974 MARCH

Onoda Hiroo, a former lieutenant of the Japanese army during the Second World War, surrenders to authorities. According to him, he continued his operations on Lubang Island because his emperor had not ordered him to surrender. President Ferdinand Marcos gives him a special pardon and warmly welcomes him to Malacañang Palace, before he finally departs for Japan.

Less than two years earlier, on 19 October 1972, one of Onoda's men, Corporal Kotsuka Kinshichi, who had also remained on Lubang Island, was shot dead in a brief encounter with the local police. President Marcos ordered a Buddhist funeral service for the soldier at the Loyola Memorial Chapel in Manila.

Before the happy event of Onoda's surrender and the tragic death of Kotsuka, it had long been reported that Japanese soldiers, not knowing that the war had ended, had been continuing operations on the island, causing harm to the inhabitants.

† 1974

The Philippines-Japan Friendship Foundation is founded. The ¥300 million seed money that made its creation possible is intended as the Japanese government's gift to President Marcos for the kind treatment he accorded the Japanese straggler Onoda, but Marcos does not accept it. Since the money cannot be returned to the Japanese coffers, former Philippine Ambassador to Japan Jose Sotero

Laurel III is persuaded to accept it and use it for the creation of the Philippines-Japan Friendship Foundation.

In 1992 the Foundation opens the Philippine Institute of Japanese Language and Culture (PIJLC) for the purpose of giving intensive lessons on Japanese language and culture to a select group of Filipinos who want to take the entrance examinations to Japanese schools and colleges.

In July 1997 the Philippines-Japan Friendship Foundation organizes the Nihongo Center Foundation and continues the work of the Nihongo Gakko of the Japan Information and Cultrual Center after the latter moved with the Japanese Embassy to its present location in Pasay City.

*1976 JULY 22

The Japanese and Philippine governments announce the official end of the reparations payment. According to the reparations treaty with Japan, ratified by the Philippine Senate in 1956, the payment period is twenty years.

*1976 NOVEMBER

The Association of Southeast Asian Nations (ASEAN) accepts Japan's proposal to establish a regular consultative forum, designed to promote a dialogue between Japan and the ASEAN.

Thus ends Japan's fear that it might forever be isolated from Southeast Asia, and Japan begins its full reentry into the region.

§1977 AUGUST 17

Japanese Prime Minister Fukuda Takeo announces in Manila the Fukuda doctrine, otherwise known as heart-to-heart diplomacy towards ASEAN. He promises to improve trade relations with the region, continue the policy of noninvolvement in military affairs, and pay more attention to cultural relations.

* 1982

Philippine Nikkei Jin kai, Incorporated (PNJK), an association of Filipino-Japanese descendants, is born. The Filipino-Japanese descendants of pre-Second World War days are called Nikkeijin. Of around 7,500 Nikkeijin in Davao, most of them third generation, about 4,000 are registered with PNJK. A primary activity of PNJK is to help the Nikkeijin trace their relatives in Japan, an important step towards being recognized as a Nikkeijin, and being able to work in Japan as unskilled workers.

In 1992, with support from a Japanese benefactor born in Davao, PNJK establishes the Mindanao Kokusai Daigaku (MDK), Mindanao International College. Initially established only for children of Nikkeijin, the MDK now accepts even those who are not Japanese descendants. Among the bachelor's degrees offered by MDK is a degree in Social Sciences, major in caregiving. Students majoring in caregiving have the opportunity to do their practicum in homes for the aged in Japan.

† 1983 May

Prime Minister Nakasone Yasuhiro visits the Philippines, the first leg of his Southeast Asian official tour. He receives a warm welcome from the public, most probably mobilized by the order of President Marcos. Nakasone expresses remorse for the sufferings caused by Japan during the Second World War.

* 1986 February

The first Philippines-Japan Friendship Month is held. The affair, which has changed appellation twice, first to Philippines-Japan Cultural Festival, and then to Philippines-Japan Festival, eventually becomes a yearly affair commencing with a grand inauguration in February, and usually extending to March or April. But since February is also the month for the commemoration of the liberation of Manila in 1945 and remembering the thousands of civilians who died, the February inauguration draws criticism from the press and Filipino intellectuals.

February 1986 is the centennial of Jose Rizal's stopover Japan on his way to Europe. The inauguration of the Philippines-Japan Festival every February is sometimes explained in terms of Rizal's sojourn in Japan. Other explanations for why the month of February has been chosen are: February is near the end of the Japanese fiscal year in March, and money allotted for cultural diplomacy has to be used up; February is a good month in the Philippines because it is not rainy and not so hot; February is spring vacation in Japan and it is easier for visiting Japanese professors and students to come to Japan.

Whatever the correct explanation, none of the above stops criticism of any Philippines-Japan celebration of friendship or cultural exchange or festival in February from appearing in newspapers, especially during the commemoration of the Battle of Manila. Neither does the criticism put a stop to the annual festival, although since the late 1990s, there has been no grand inauguration of the annual festival in February.

On 7 June 2005 President Gloria M. Arroyo issues Proclamation Number 854, declaring Sunday, July 23, 2006 as Philippines-Japan Friendship Day. The day marks the fiftieth anniversary of the ratification of the San Francisco Treaty and the normalization of Philippines-Japan relations. In 2007, the year following the proclamation, it is announced that the celebration of the Philippines-Japan festival will begin in July rather than February. However, cultural events featuring Japan have been announced and held since January of that year.

1986 NOVEMBER 10–13

President Corazon Aquino makes a state visit to Japan and meets with the emperor and Prime Minister Nakasone Yasuhiro.

After her courtesy call on the Japanese Emperor, Press Secretary Teodoro Benigno tells the press that the Emperor repeatedly apologized to Aquino for the actions of the Japanese soldiers during the

Second World War. The Imperial Household Agency denies the story; the Japanese Ministry of Foreign Affairs refuses to comment on it, on the ground that according to longstanding rules, the content of conversations between the Emperor and his foreign guests should not be made public.

During Aquino's meeting with Prime Minister Nakasone, the latter assures her that Japan will support the Philippines' efforts at economic reconstruction. Nakasone pledges a special US$252.5 million loan apart from the usual ODA loan package.

On 12 November, Waseda University confers an honorary doctorate degree on Aquino.

1986 November 15

Wakaoji Nobuyuki, head of the Manila branch of Mitsui and Company, is abducted on his way home from the Canlubang Golf and Country Club. After four months, he is released in the evening of 31 May 1987 near Santo Domingo Church in Quezon City.

To date, the identity of his abductors and whether ransom has been paid have not yet been established. But during his captivity, Philippines-Japan relations suffer setbacks, albeit merely on the level of perceptions: The Japanese government imposes a ban on Japanese travel to the Philippines; Japanese and Philippine mass media accuse the Aquino government of incompetence and inefficiency; Philippine media also accuses the Japanese government of high-handed tactics to force the Aquino government to solve the case; some conjure up memories of Japanese brutalities during the Second World War and still others remind the public of the way Japanese yakuza maltreat Filipino workers in Japan.

*1989 January 7

Emperor Hirohito of Japan dies. On 23 February President Corazon Aquino leaves on a regular Philippine Airlines flight to Tokyo to attend his funeral.

† 1989 JULY 3-5

The Multilateral Aid Initiative (MAI), more popularly known in the Philippines as the Philippine Assistance Program (PAP), is formally launched in Tokyo. The program, conceived by the United States in 1987, and which is under the overall coordination of the World Bank, aims to coordinate multilateral aid to the Philippines.

Under MAI, five geographical areas are identified for special development projects (SDP). They are CALABARZON (Cavite, Laguna, Batangas, Rizal, Quezon), Panay/Negros and Samar in the Visayas, and Cagayan de Oro and South Cotabato/General Santos in Mindanao.

* 1990 AUGUST 7

Carlos B. Teraoka, a sixty-four year old Filipino businessman of Japanese descent from Baguio City is appointed honorary consul of Japan, the first Asian and the first Filipino to receive such an appointment.

The honor and responsibility bestowed on Teraoka signify the Japanese government's recognition of the descendants of Japanese immigrants who first came to the Mountain Province in 1903.

† 1992 JANUARY

Reports about how the Japanese military officially compelled some Filipino women to give sexual services to Japanese soldiers during the Second World War begin to appear in the newspapers. The Japanese government conducts an investigation and in July admits that the Japanese Imperial Army established "comfort stations" in several Asian countries it occupied during the Second World War.

In the Philippines, the Task Force on Filipino Comfort Women and the National Commission on the Role of Filipino Women call on former comfort women to come out in the open. Maria Rosa Henson

Luna is the first to come out. In 1993, Maria and five more women file a class-action suit against the Japanese government and demand compensation and an official apology. The Task Force on Filipino Comfort Women also demands inclusion of the comfort-women story during the Second World War in Japanese textbooks.

† 1992 FEBRUARY

The Japan International Cooperation Agency (JICA) hands over to the Philippine government the master plan for the industrial development of CALABARZON (Cavite, Laguna, Batangas, Rizal, and Quezon) provinces which constitute Region IV-A of the Philippines, one of the five designated regions for industrial development under MAI launched in Tokyo in July 1989. The Philippine government has requested JICA to prepare the Master Plan. JICA in turn requests Nippon Koei (Japan Engineering) Company, the biggest aid consultant company in Japan, to draw up the plan. The final report under the name of JICA is finished in October 1991 and is handed to the Philippine government in February 1992.

† 1993 MARCH 9-14

Philippine President Fidel Ramos visits Japan. One of the accomplishments of the visit is a comprehensive economic assistance to the Philippines totaling US$1.2 billion.

§ 1993 AUGUST 4

The Japanese government, through Chief Cabinet Secretary Kono Yohei, publicly admits that the Japanese Imperial Army has been involved in the establishment of quarters called "comfort stations" for the sexual needs of the Japanese soldiers during the Second World War.

† 1994 AUGUST 23–25

Japanese Prime Minister Murayama Tomiichi visits the Philippines. Murayama apologizes for Japanese atrocities during the Second World War. In connection with issues related to the comfort women, he offers to fund through ODA a job training center for women.

† 1995 JULY 19

The Asian Women's Fund (AWF) is established. The AWF is Japan's response to the demands by the comfort women in Asian countries occupied by Japan during the Second World War for an apology and compensation from the Japanese government. The organization raises the money from contributions from private corporations and the general public to compensate the women.

By the time it is dissolved on 31 March 2007, the AWF has disbursed a total of ¥17 billion, 565 million of which consists of private donations, and 1.12 billion in state funds. Private donations have been distributed to individual comfort women as atonement money, while state funds have been used for medical and welfare support for the women.

Because the so-called "atonement money" does not come from the Japanese government, some comfort women have refused to accept it. They and their supporters have accused the Japanese government of using the AWF to avoid offering an official apology and using government money to compensate them.

* 1996 JUNE 18

Japan Foundation, established in 1971, opens its eighteenth overseas branch in Manila. The Japan Foundation is the principal agency of the Japanese government for the promotion of Japanese language and culture all over the world. The establishment of a branch in Manila in 1996 attests to the importance Japan gives to the Philippines and the mileage

Japanese cultural policy towards the Philippines has gained since the opening of the Japan Information and Cultural Center in the 1960s.

† 1996 August 16

A letter from Japanese Prime Minister Hashimoto Ryutaro and atonement money of ¥2 million each (about 400,000 pesos at the current exchange rate) are presented to Maria Rosa Henson Luna, Anastasia Cortes, and Rufina Fernandez, from the Asian Women's Fund, in the presence of Japanese ambassador Yushita Hiroyuki. By July 1997eighteen Filipino women have received compensation from the AWF. The letter, written in Japanese, English, and Tagalong, reads: "I extend anew my most sincere apology and remorse to all the women who underwent immeasurable and painful experiences and suffered incurable physical and psychological wounds as comfort women."

† 1999 February 16

Prince Akishino and Princess Kiko arrive for a five-day visit in connection with the centennial celebration of the declaration of Philippine independence in 1899. The Japanese government takes the centennial celebration as an opportunity to reinforce its cultural diplomacy in the Philippines.

1999 December 4

A newspaper reports that Antonio Cerilles, Secretary of the Department of Environment and Natural Resources, orders the filing of charges against officials of Sinsei Enterprise and Macondray Carriers and Brokerage Corporation for smuggling some 60,000 tons of garbage from Japan. Cerilles explains that the hazardous wastes can be considered illegal under the Basel Convention since there was no prior notification and consent from the Philippine government.

On 21 December the seven-member Japanese team of environmental and health experts and top government officials arrives to verify if the tons of garbage imported from Japan which are rotting at the Manila South Harbor are indeed hazardous wastes. The following day Ishii Masafumi, director of the Southeast Asian Division of the Japanese Foreign Ministry, and head of the Japanese team, acknowledges that the 100 containers of wastes are indeed hazardous and are from Japan. They are wastes from medical centers, hospitals and clinics.

*2000 April 16

The Manila Japanese School opens classes in its new location at the Bonifacio Global City. It used to occupy the second floor of the Filinvest Building on Taft Avenue. The Japan Information and Cultural Center is on the first floor. At first, the Manila Japanese School was not officially recognized by the Philippine government. After its official recognition, it moved to Parañaque City, where it remained for about twenty years, before moving to the Bonifacio Global City. The school's present location in the sprawling, modern Bonifacio Global City attests to the stability and growth of the Japanese expatriate community in the Philippines.

†2001 September 13

During President Gloria Arroyo's visit to Japan, she and Prime Minister Koizumi Junichiro jointly condemn terrorist attacks on the United States on 11 September (more popularly known as 9/11), and pledge their utmost cooperation with the United States in fighting terrorism.

†2002 May 20

Waseda University confers upon President Gloria M. Arroyo the Doctor of Laws degree, honoris causa.

2003 MAY 30

Japanese Ambassador to the Philippines Takano Kojiro apologizes for the undiplomatic comments he made about the peace and order situation in the Philippines. He had remarked to the Foreign Correspondents Association of the Philippines that Japanese investors do not come to the Philippines because of the unsatisfactory peace and order situation. What he described as the scary situation even caused him sleepless nights, he added. The apology comes after the Philippine government's protest against the "exaggerated" remark, and criticism from mass media. On the other hand, some commentators, while admitting that the remark is undiplomatic, say that the ambassador only spoke the truth, and that it is a wakeup call to the Philippine government.

On 24 October 2004 the new ambassador to the Philippines, Yamazaki Ryuichiro, arrives to assume the position vacated by Takano.

§2005 FEBRUARY 3

Alberto Romulo, Secretary of Foreign Affairs, arrives in Tokyo to ask Japan to stop its plan to impose stricter requirements for entertainer visas. After the United States State Department castigated Japan in 2002 for its failure to stop human trafficking, the Japanese government responds by granting entertainer visas only to applicants who have had at least two years of experience as artists outside of Japan, or training in foreign educational institutions. Since the announcement, the Japanese Embassy in Manila has been the scene of regular protest demonstrations by entertainers, recruiters, and their supporters.

Nonetheless, on 15 February, the Japanese government enacts the revised, stricter visa requirement, to take effect a month later on 15 March. By the end of August, the Philippine Overseas Employment Agency (POEA) estimates that the deployment of overseas performing artists to Japan has dropped by 38.46 percent. Concretely, it means that from January to July of the year, only 23,359 entertainers are hired from the Philippines, 15,000 fewer than the recorded 37,958 deployed during the same period in the previous year.

† 2005 OCTOBER 23

The Manila International Sister Cities Association Incorporated (MISCA) brings to Yokohama, sister city of Manila, the Philippines' traditional Santacruzan. Philippine beauties (called *sagala* in Tagalog) with their handsome escorts parade on the streets of Isezaki-cho, Yokohama.

The event is primarily an attempt to attract Japanese tourists to the Philippines. The sister-city relationship between Yokohama and Manila dates back to 1965, it being one of the first sister-city tie-ups between the Philippines and Japan. Promotion of tourism is one of the aims of the sister-city relationship. Very few Japanese understand the meaning of santacruzan, but what may have inspired MISCA to do it in Yokokama is the presence of many Filipino overseas workers in Japan who appreciate it and may even explain it to their Japanese acquaintances and friends. This Santacruzan, in other words, is not only for the promotion of tourism, but also to bring joy to the Filipino community in Yokohama.

* 2006 SEPTEMBER 9

In Helsinki President Gloria M. Arroyo and Prime Minister Koizumi Junichiro sign the Japan-Philippines Economic Partnership Agreement (JPEPA). The agreement includes free-trade provisions on various export and import items as well as entry of Filipino nurses and caregivers to Japan. JPEPA is the first economic partnership agreement signed by Japan that includes an item on entry of workers to Japan. On 17 November President Arroyo submits the agreement to the Philippine Senate, the body that has the authority to ratify international treaties entered into by the Philippine government.

The fiftieth anniversary of the normalization of Philippines-Japan relations—23 July 2006—has been targeted as the date for the signing, and Prime Minister Koizumi has been scheduled to come to Manila to make the signing a special feature of the anniversary celebration. Due to difficulties in the negotiations, particularly the issues on Philippine agricultural products, Japanese cars, and entry of Filipino nurses and caregivers to Japan, the signing is delayed, causing the cancellation of Koizumi's visit to the Philippines.

Regarding Philippine exports to Japan, the resumption of exporting filter-smoked tuna to Japan is widely considered one of the first test cases of JPEPA. Japan has imposed a ban since 1997 on smoked tuna from the Philippines, claiming that they do not pass Japan's food-safety laws.

Still another problem to be solved is how many Filipino nurses and caregivers will actually be able to get a license to work in Japan for a period longer than three or four years (which is only for trainees), given the strict requirements imposed by the Japanese government. Passing a quite high level of Japanese language proficiency examination and the licensing test for nurses is part of the requirements.

A problem that may possibly delay, if not prevent, the ratification of the agreement is a provision that allows Japan to export hazardous wastes to the Philippines. The provision has attracted a great amount of criticism in the press.

† 2006 DECEMBER 8

Japanese Prime Minister Abe Shinzo arrives in Manila, originally to attend the Twelfth ASEAN Summit in Cebu, but since it has been postponed due to "an approaching big typhoon" according to the Philippine government, Abe just stays in Manila and holds talks with President Gloria M. Arroyo. The summit is eventually held on 9 to 15 January 2007 and Prime Minister Abe attends it, despite earlier speculations that he may not be able to.

Among the topics taken up in the talks between Abe and Arroyo in Manila are the continuation of Japanese loans, grants, and investments to the Philippines, the introduction of development assistance to the Mindanao peace process, and the Japanese concern over alleged human rights violations and political killings in the Philippines.

The following day, 9 December, Arroyo and Abe inaugurate the third-generation (3G) trains of the Light Rail Transit Authority. The new phase of the light rail transit consists of forty-eight fully airconditioned cars, augmenting the existing sixty-three first-generation and twenty-eight second-generation light rail cars. It is funded by a loan of 8.893 billion pesos from Japan, payable in thirty years at the rate of 1 percent interest a year.

In the morning of the same day, Japan and the Philippines sign three documents: The Philippines-Japan Joint Statement: Partnership Between Close Neighbors for Comprehensive Cooperation, signed by Arroyo and Abe; Exchange of Notes on the Pasig-Marikina River Channel Improvement Project, signed by Foreign Affairs Undersecretary Franklin Ebdalin and Japanese Ambassador Yamazaki Ryuichiro; Protocol Amending the Convention between Japan and the Philippines for the Avoidance of Double Taxation and the Prevention of Fiscal Evasion with respect to taxes on income, signed by the Japanese ambassador and Finance Secretary Margarito Teves.

§2006 DECEMBER 9

Japan presents to the Philippines the Japan Bangsamoro Initiatives for Reconstruction and Development (J-BIRD) as part of Japan's contribution to the ongoing Mindanao Peace Process. The presentation is done during the visit of Prime Minister Abe to the Philippines, after the signing ceremony of three documents, one of them the joint statement by Abe and President Gloria M. Arroyo on "Partnership Between Close Neighbors for Comprehensive Cooperation." The joint statement consists of several commitments, and Japan's decision to help in the development of Mindanao and the peace process is one of them.

Prior to the presentation, and as preparation for Japan's decision to have a role in the Mindanao peace process, Yamada Shigeo, director of the Second Southeast Asia Division of the Japanese Ministry of Foreign Affairs, and Ishikawa Yoshihisa, first secretary of the political section of the Japanese Embassy in Manila, hold talks with the Mindanao Liberation Front (MILF) in its satellite office in Simuay, Sultan Kudarat, Maguindanao on 7 May to signify Japan's intention to play an active role in the International Monitoring Team (IMT). The IMT, composed of Malaysia, Brunei, and Libya has been operating in Mindanao since October 2004 after the Philippine government and MILF agreed on a ceasefire in July 2003.

On 23 July, on the occasion of the fiftieth anniversary of the normalization of Philippines-Japan relations, Foreign Minister Aso Taro of Japan informs President Arroyo of Japan's decision to dispatch a development expert to the IMT's socio-economic monitoring, which is one of the pillars of IMT's mandate. The other pillar is ceasefire monitoring. The Japanese development expert will be stationed at the IMT headquarters in Davao City.

The Authors

Lydia N. Yu Jose, professor of Political Science at the Ateneo de Manila University, is currently the executive director of the Ateneo Center for Asian Studies. She obtained her Ph.D. in International Relations from Sophia University in Japan. She was a visiting professor at the Tokyo University of Foreign Studies from 2001 to 2002. Among her major publications are *Japan Views the Philippines* (Ateneo de Manila University Press) and *Filipinos in Japan and Okinawa* (Tokyo University of Foreign Studies).

Ricardo Trota Jose, professor of History at the University of the Philippines, Diliman, obtained his Ph.D. from the Tokyo University of Foreign Studies. He specializes in military and diplomatic history, with focus on the Japanese occupation of the Philippines. Among his major publications are *The Philippine Army, 1935–1942* (Ateneo de Manila University Press,) and volume seven (on the Japanese Occupation) of the multi-volume *Kasaysayan* (Readers' Digest).

Cecilia P. Tolentino, currently the President of the Association of Philippine Private Alumni of Japanese Universities (APPAJU), Treasurer of the Philippine Federation of Japan Alumni (PHILFEJA), and adviser of the Philippine Association of the Japanese Government

Scholars (PHILAJAMES), Incorporated, finished her Bachelor of Science in Foreign Service at the University of the Philippines and proceeded to Waseda University in Japan to take up Japanese Studies courses on an Asia Foundation scholarship. She worked at the Japan Information and Cultural Center from its opening in 1967 until her retirement, serving for thirty eight years. On 29 April 2004 the emperor of Japan conferred on her the "Order of the Sacred Treasure, Gold and Silver Rays" for her contribution to the promotion of mutual understanding and friendship between the Philippines and Japan.

Mari-Jo P. Ruiz, professor of Mathematics at the Ateneo de Manila University, received a research grant from the Japan Society for the Promotion of Science in 1983. Since then, she has worked with Japanese mathematicians on research in Graph Theory, organizing conferences in the Asian region, and conceptualizing exhibitions to promote public awareness of mathematics. She was part of the group that founded the journal *Graphs and Combinatorics.*

Senga Kunio, Currently Director-General, South Asia Department of the Asian Development Bank (ADB), was born in Tokyo. After graduating from high school, he came to Manila to take up Economics at the Ateneo de Manila University. After completing his degree, he proceeded with his post-graduate studies at the School of Economics, University of the Philippines. He worked briefly at the International Labor Organization, before joining ADB as one of the first Young Professionals.

Alely Alejar-Bernardo, Currently Senior Results Management Officer, South Asia Department, ADB, obtained her master's degree from the National Graduate Institute for Policy Studies in Japan, through a Japanese government scholarship. She was a visiting research fellow at the Japan Institute for International Affairs, a think tank of the Japanese Ministry of Foreign Affairs, and the Graduate School of Economics, Nagoya University. Prior to joining ADB, she worked with the Public Investment Staff of the National Economic Development Authority, in charge of Japanese ODA and other multilateral and bilateral development cooperation programs.

Satake Masaaki, professor of Sociology at Nagoya Gakuin University, obtained his Ph.D. in International Relations from Sophia University in Japan. He was a visiting research associate in the Institute of Philippine Culture, Ateneo de Manila University, from 1987 to 1989 and again from 1997 to 1998. Among his major works is *People's Economy: Philippine Community-Based Industries and Alternative Development* (Solidaridad Publishing House). An upcoming publication is *Nippi Kekkon to Tabunka-kyosei: Beer, Lechon and Bamboo Dance* [Filipino-Japanese Intermarriages and Multicultural Cohabitation: Beer, Lechon and Bamboo Dance], coauthored with Mary Angeline Da-anoy, his wife.

Efren Ed. C. Flores, currently president of the Foundation for Alternative Management of the Environment, finished his Master of Science in Fisheries at Nagasaki University, and his Doctor of Science in Fisheries at Hokkaido University. He was Dean of the College of Fisheries from 1986 to 1992 and was later seconded to the Southeast Asian Fisheries Development Center as Chief of the Aquaculture Department from 1992 to 1996. From 1992 to 2002 he served as team leader of a group of specialists on an ADB-JBIC funded project on fisheries management in the Bureau of Fisheries and Aquatic Resources. He met his wife Yamamoto Yoko in Japan and married her in 1972.

Tito Genova Valiente teaches courses in Japanese cinema at the Ateneo de Manila University. He used to be a columnist of *Today*, and currently maintains a column with the *Business Mirror*, writing mostly on films. In 1986, he was in Rikkyo University under the Ateneo de Manila-Rikkyo Exchange Program and again, in 1990, as a Research Scholar of the Japanese Government. He was a Japan

Foundation Fellow in 2004. He serves as consultant for research on women in development by various NGOs and for cultural studies with the UNICEF (in cooperation with the Cultural Center of the Philippines).

Ronaldo L. Santos, Jr. is currently taking up law in the University of the Philippines. He obtained his Bachelor of Arts, major in Political Science, from the Ateneo de Manila University in 2005.

Junefe Gilig Payot obtained his Bachelor of Arts, major in Economics, and Master of Arts, major in Japanese Studies from the Ateneo de Manila University. He teaches a Japanese language and culture course in the same university. He studied as an exchange student at the Kansai Gaidai University in Osaka and at Rikkyo University in Tokyo. He became interested in Japanese NGOs because of his own involvement in social development work as a researcher on urban poverty and governance at the John J. Carroll Institute on Church and Social Issues where he has been working since 2001.

Index